How to care for your
Flowering Houseplants

Series editor: David Longman

Colour illustrations by Stuart Lafford

How to care for your
Flowering
Houseplants

by Tom Gough and David Longman

Peter Lowe

THE AUTHORS

Tom Gough trained in horticulture with the famous houseplant
growers, Thomas Rochford and studied floristry both in Britain
and the Netherlands. He is chairman of Interflora, Greater
London and a director of a London florist company. David
Longman trained at the Royal Horticultural Society's school at
Wisley before joining his family firm of florists. He is council
member of Interflora, a director of the Flower and Plant Council
and a regular exhibitor at the Chelsea Flower Show. He is
General Editor of this series.

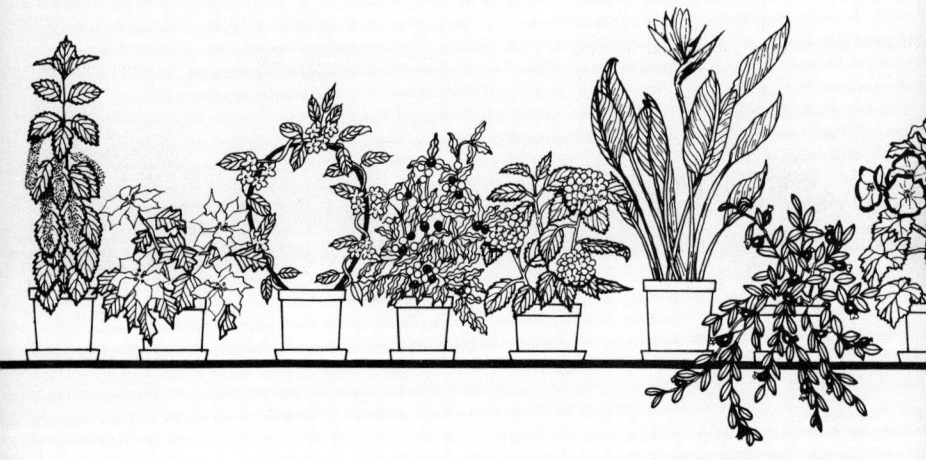

ISBN 0 85654 636 4

Printed in Italy by New Interlitho SpA

Contents

Scientific names

Introduction

How to use this book

Most people have at one time either bought or been given a flowering plant and been disappointed when their new possession, healthy and beautiful in the garden centre or supermarket, begins to droop and fade. This book, one of two volumes on flowering houseplants in a comprehensive houseplant series, is here to help you.

It describes the flowering houseplants that you are likely to find in shops, garden centres – even motorway service stations. Each plant has a self-contained two-page entry. On the left is a general description of the plant with details of how to look after it, giving the correct amounts of water, light, warmth and humidity it needs, explaining how to clean and repot it and when and if it needs pruning. There is also a colour photo of a healthy leaf or flower. On the right-hand page is a colour illustration of the plant showing all the things than can go wrong with it. Since this picture shows all the troubles at once, some of the plants look very sick indeed! To find out what is wrong with your plant, look for its symptoms in the illustration. Read the caption next to the part of the picture that shows the same features as your plant. It tells you what is wrong and how to put it right.

Different plants require different care and conditions. The cyclamen, for example, soon wilts if it is overwatered or kept in too hot a place. The poinsettia, on the other hand, likes warmth and humidity and needs to have moist compost at all times while it is in flower. Most flowering plants need more light than other houseplants if they are to produce a good crop of flowers but not all require high temperatures and many must actually be shaded from direct sunlight. So whether you are beginning with a familiar Busy Lizzie or progressing to an exotic orchid or a miniature orange tree, make sure you read the detailed care instructions for your plant and you will be able to look after it with confidence.

Tools for indoor gardening

It is possible to look after plants with the minimum of equipme a watering can, sprayer and plastic sponge are the real esse However, for long-term houseplant care, you will need a muc more comprehensive collection, which can be acquired grad as the need arises.

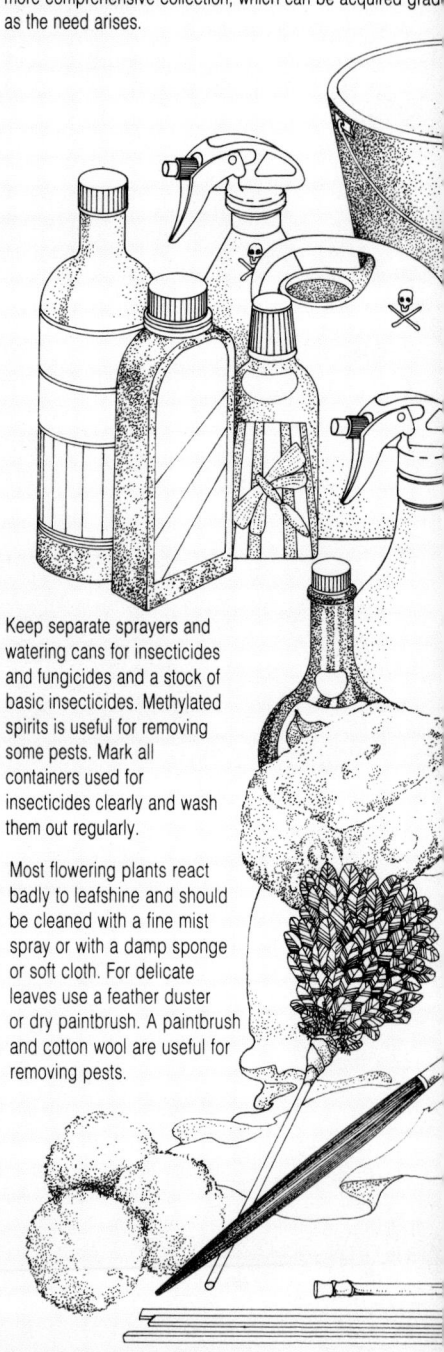

Keep separate sprayers and watering cans for insecticides and fungicides and a stock of basic insecticides. Methylated spirits is useful for removing some pests. Mark all containers used for insecticides clearly and wash them out regularly.

Most flowering plants react badly to leafshine and should be cleaned with a fine mist spray or with a damp sponge or soft cloth. For delicate leaves use a feather duster or dry paintbrush. A paintbrush and cotton wool are useful for removing pests.

A small garden trowel and fork are useful when repotting or adding topsoil. A large spoon is a good substitute. A plastic bucket is essential for mixing composts, wetting peat and for giving very dry plants a thorough soaking.

Keep a selection of loam-based and peat-based composts, some pure moss or sedge peat. Some plants require lime-free mixtures. Sharp sand can be obtained from garden centres. Fertilizer, hormone rooting powder and charcoal are all useful.

Scissors, secateurs and a sharp knife are useful for removing dead or damaged fronds.

Two watering cans to which a rose can be attached are useful, one pint (½ litre) size, the other holding about a gallon (4½l). Never use your normal watering can for insecticides or fungicides.

Keep a small stock of flower pots and saucers, both plastic and clay. Old clay flower pots can be broken up to make excellent drainage material. Outer pots, with no drainage holes, can be used to hide the standard pot.

Twine, string, raffia and plant rings are essential for climbing plants, with a selection of canes, sticks and moss poles.

7

Watering and spraying

More houseplants are killed by incorrect watering (mainly of the little and often variety) than by anything else. Most prefer to be given a good soaking, then left almost to dry out before they are watered again. Some must be kept always moist – but in these cases the pot must be well drained so that the roots do not become waterlogged. Others prefer to dry out more thoroughly between waterings. Some need more water at one time of year than another. Always test the compost before watering to see how dry it is below the surface. In cold weather do not use cold water straight from the tap or the shock may damage the plant. Use tepid water for both watering and spraying.

Spraying keeps a plant's leaves clean and also provides extra humidity in hot, dry rooms. Avoid tap water if possible as the lime it contains clogs the pores of the leaves. Rainwater collected in a tank or bucket, water from melted ice in the freezer or boiled water which has been allowed to cool are all more suitable. Do not spray in bright sunlight as the water acts like a magnifying glass and may cause burn or scorch marks. A few plants dislike water on their leaves so before spraying you should check the individual requirements under each plant entry. Most, however benefit from a fine mist spray.

Feeding

Most composts contain fertilizer but for healthy growth plants also need extra nourishment, usually in spring and summer. Houseplant food or fertilizer is available as a liquid, diluted before use, as a powder added to water, as granules scattered on the surface of the soil and as a pill or stick pushed into the soil and gradually absorbed. You can also obtain a foliar feed which is sprayed onto the leaves. For most houseplants a liquid food is most suitable. It is clean, has no smell, and is easy and economical to use. There are several brands available and it is a good idea to try several and to change from time to time. Normally you can simply follow the instructions on the

Watering

1. Test compost for dryness with finger or knife blade before watering. If blade comes out clean or soil dry and crumbly, compost is drying out. If soil sticks, it is still moist. Check instructions for each plant: some like a dry interval, others must be always moist.

2. Add water to top of compost, filling pot to the brim. Excess water will drain into saucer. After 15 minutes, empty any water remaining in the saucer. Do not allow pot to stand in water.

3. If plant is very dried out and does not mind water on its leaves, plunge pot into bowl so that water covers pot rim. Spray leaves. Leave for 15 minutes, then take it out and allow it to drain.

4. If plant cannot tolerate water on its leaves, add water to fill the saucer and wait for 15 minutes for it to be absorbed. Empty excess so plant does not stand in water. Or, plunge pot into bowl or bucket of water to just below pot rim. Leave for 15 minutes, then take out and allow to drain.

5. Bromeliads such as the Urn plant *(Aechmea fasciata)* need to have water in their central well. Use rainwater if possible and renew after 3 weeks if not absorbed.

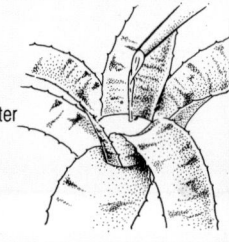

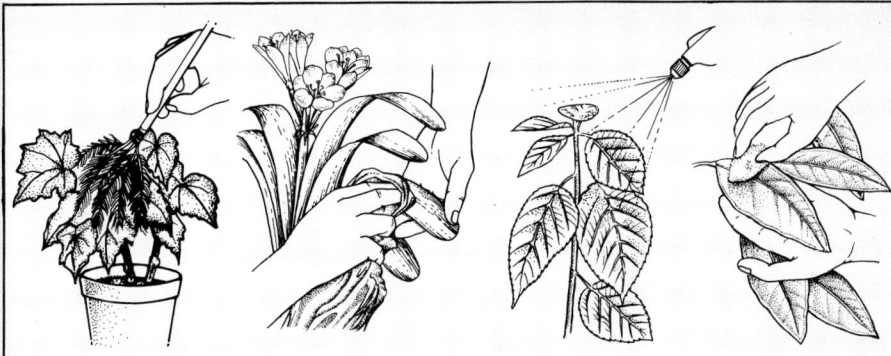

Cleaning the leaves
1. Flick very dusty plants with a feather duster before cleaning.

2. Wipe larger leaves with a damp cloth or sponge to remove dust and any insects such as red spider mite. Use soft water if possible. Remember to wipe the undersides of the leaves as well as the tops.

3. Spraying (with soft water if possible) is often enough to keep plants clean. The lime in hard tap water may mark the leaves and clog the pores. Do not spray the flowers and do not spray in sunlight.

4. Very few flowering plants tolerate leafshine on their leaves as they are easily burned or clogged by the oils it contains. Check instructions and never use more than once a month.

Humidity
Some flowering plants require higher humidity than is found in normal rooms, especially in dry, centrally heated homes. A group of plants will create its own more humid atmosphere but you can improve the humidity around them in several ways.

1. Spray regularly with soft water, holding spray about 6in (15cm) from plant. Do not spray in strong sunlight. Spray may mark or rot flowers, so check plant's requirements when in flower.

2. Put pebbles in plant's saucer and stand pot on top. Add water to saucer until it comes half way up the pebbles. Do not let bottom of pot touch water or plant will become waterlogged and roots will rot away. Water vapour will rise from the damp pebbles, providing extra humidity under the leaves. Add more water to saucer when pebbles begin to dry. A group of plants can be placed together on a tray of damp pebbles for even better local humidity.

3. Place pot inside a larger container and pack the space between the two with damp peat. Keep peat constantly moist. This is a good method to use if you have to leave the plants for some time as the peat will hold moisture well.

Pruning
Old flowering plants may grow straggly and produce fewer flowers. Pruning back leggy stems in spring encourages new side shoots which in turn produce more flowers. In general, cut stems down by half, just above a leaf or side shoot. But read individual instructions as some must never be pruned.

Cut off dead flowers so that plant's energy goes to new buds and leaves.

bottle, adding a few drops to the water in the can when watering. For some plants, however, the mixture must be weaker than the manufacturer recommends on the bottle. If it is used at too concentrated a strength, it will damage the roots. Never increase the recommended strength and be careful with tablets and fertilizer sticks. If they are too close to the roots, the concentrated fertilizer may cause root damage.

If in doubt, don't feed. It is always better to slightly underfeed than to overfeed – and never feed a sick plant.

Repotting

Plants need repotting either because the roots have totally filled the existing pot and can no longer develop or because the nutritional value of the compost has been used up. It's quite easy to tell if a plant needs repotting. Remove it from its pot (see right). If there is a mass of roots and no soil showing, it needs repotting – it is potbound. If any soil is visible, don't repot. Replace plant in its old pot and gently firm it back in position. Other signs are roots growing through the pot base and weak, slow growth. Newly purchased plants should not normally need repotting. Do not repot unhealthy plants: the shock may kill them. In fact if in doubt, don't repot.

Repotting is usually done in spring – March or April in the northern hemisphere, September or October in the southern. Most plants require good drainage so that water can run through the compost freely and air can get to its roots. Broken crocks from old clay flower pots or a layer of coarse gravel at the bottom of the pot will provide drainage. Never use a container without drainage holes in its base. Put a piece of paper or a layer of moss over the drainage crocks to stop the compost from blocking the holes and inspect the root ball for pests. Remove old stones, damaged roots and old soil and gently remove old, loose compost from the top to a depth of about ½in (1cm). Then place plant in new pot.

After repotting, leave the plant without water for 2–3 days. The roots will spread out into the new compost in search of water. If it

is very hot, spray the leaves every day.

Choosing the right compost: The correct type of compost or soil is very important for indoor plants. Don't use ordinary soil, which is usually too heavy and stifles the roots of young plants. Compost types vary considerably as some houseplants need a very light peat-based compost and some a heavy loam. The correct combination for each plant is given in the individual entries.

The two most commonly used types of compost are loam-based or peat-based. Loam-based compost is made up of sterilized loam (soil) mixed with peat and grit or coarse, washed sand. It is usually sold with fertilizer added, following formulae developed by the John Innes Institute for Horticultural Research. The numbers 1, 2 and 3 indicate the different proportions of fertilizer added. In this book they are refer-

---

Dividing tubers

Flowering plants such as Gloxinias have underground tubers which can be divided in spring as they start to bud.

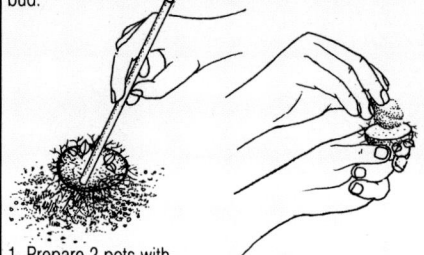

1. Prepare 2 pots with drainage, compost and an inch (2½cm) sharp sand. Remove tuber from pot and remove stale soil.

3. Dust cut ends with sulphur dust to prevent fungal infection.

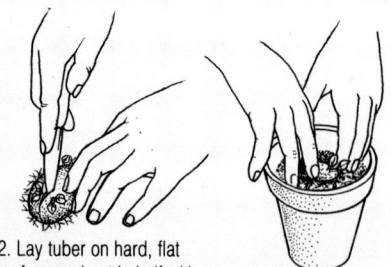

2. Lay tuber on hard, flat surface and cut in half with a sharp knife. Each section must include a shoot and roots.

4. Pot each section separately with half the tuber above the compost.

10

Taking cuttings

This is the most common way of propagating houseplants though seeds of some species are available. First prepare a small pot with drainage and special rooting compost.

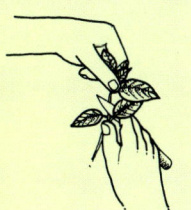

3. Dust the cut ends with hormone rooting powder.

5. Place in heated propagator or cover with polythene and keep in warm place (70°F, 21°C). Keep watered and remove cover for 5 minutes a day.

6. When cuttings begin to grow (in about 4 weeks), pot singly in small pots.

1. Choose a healthy stem tip or side stem and cut off the top 3–4in (8–10cm). Cuttings should include a growing tip and 2 pairs of healthy leaves.

2. Remove lowest pair of leaves and any side shoots from bottom part so there is a length of bare stem to insert into compost. Prepare other cuttings in the same way.

4. Make holes around edge of new pot. Insert several cuttings and firm compost gently round them. Water well.

Offsets

Bromeliads such as Flaming sword *(Vriesia)* produce offsets which can be separated from the parent plant when they are about half its size and have their own root system.

5. Lower plant into new pot and add more compost round root ball, firming it with fingers or a round stick. Continue adding compost until pot is filled to within ½–¾in (1–1½cm). Leave for 3 days without water in shade.

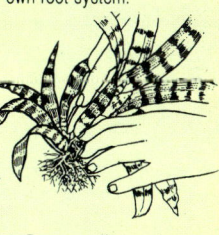

1. Remove offset and roots from parent plant with sharp knife.

Repotting

1. Prepare clean, dry pot not more than 2 sizes larger than old one. Place broken crocks or coarse gravel in bottom as drainage, then a piece of paper or moss and layer of new compost. Water plant well.

3. Remove damaged or dead roots with sharp knife.

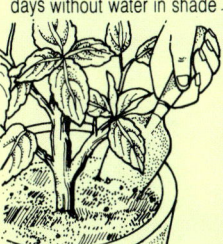

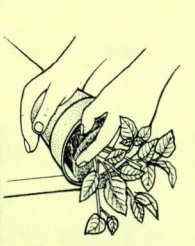

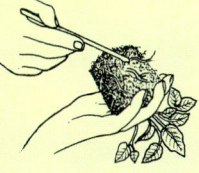

2. Hold pot upside down as shown. Gently tap rim of pot on edge of table and remove pot with other hand. If pot sticks, tap in several places.

4. Gently break roots at bottom of ball and remove any bits of crock or stone. Remove all loose, old compost from top, to a depth of about ½in (1cm). Always handle with care so as not to damage leaves or buds.

6. For large plants in tubs carefully scrape away about 2–3in (5–7cm) old topsoil. Add new compost, leaving ½–¾in (1–1½cm) space between compost and pot rim. Firm down well and water, including feed.

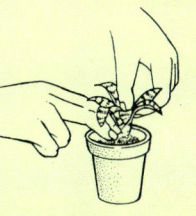

2. Pot offset in new pot, firming compost around base. Water plant well. Keep warm (75°F (24°C)).

11

Growing from seed

1. Prepare seed tray or propagator with drainage and seed compost. Make shallow furrow and sow seed evenly along it. Cover with thin layer of compost no thicker than depth of seed itself.

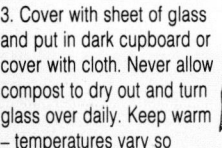

2. Spray compost with water until it is evenly moist. Use mist spray or fine rose attached to watering can. Do not flood with water.

3. Cover with sheet of glass and put in dark cupboard or cover with cloth. Never allow compost to dry out and turn glass over daily. Keep warm – temperatures vary so check instructions on seed packet.

4. When seeds begin to sprout, bring into light and remove glass cover. Continue to water regularly. Do not feed.

5. When seedlings are large enough to handle, thin out the weaker ones, leaving about 1in (2½cm) between each one.

6. When plants have grown at least 2 leaves in addition to their first seedling leaves, repot each one in a small pot with normal compost. Firm compost around them well. Feed with liquid houseplant food diluted to a quarter recommended strength every 3 weeks.

Lighting

1. If plants are in too dark a corner they will not grow well and will turn their leaves and flower stems in the direction of the brightest light.

2. Full sunlight may damage leaves or flowers. Shade from direct midday sun with a fine gauze curtain. This will filter and diffuse the light. A plant placed opposite a white wall which faces the sun will also benefit from diffused light.

3. Horticultural spotlights have blue-tinted reflector bulbs which imitate sunlight. If using fluorescent tubes, put one tinted horticultural tube with a normal one to give best light.

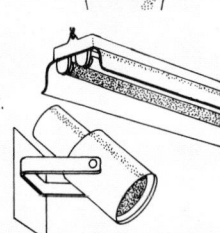

Shading a greenhouse

Midday summer sun in a greenhouse is too strong for some houseplants. Stretch horizontal wires above plants and hang fine shading netting over to protect them.

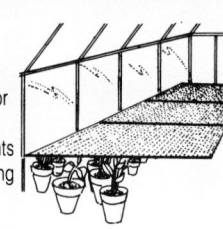

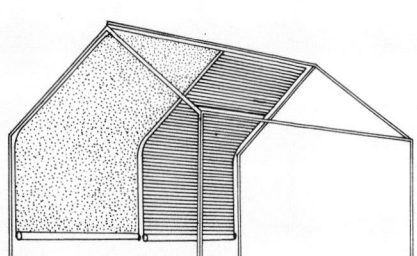

The best, but most expensive way of providing shade is to fit adjustable roller blinds made from wooden slats or thin material. These can be moved easily and do not restrict access to the plants. Your local garden centre will advise you.

Finally, the easiest, cheapest way is to spray the outside with powdered shading paint mixed with water. This may wash off in the rain and must be removed in winter or light will be too dim.

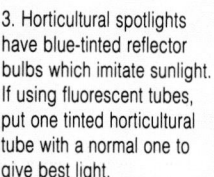

12

red to as 'loam-based No. 1, 2 or 3'. They are especially good for larger plants as they give more stability.

Peat-based composts are more open in texture, sterile, and hold moisture longer. They are normally composed of 10 parts of peat to 1 part of coarse sand with fertilizer added in the same proportions as loam-based compost. It is important when using peat composts not to firm them into the pot too hard. Plants absorb the fertilizer content more quickly from these composts than from loam-based ones.

Ericaceous or lime-free compost is available for plants that do not tolerate lime. Sphagnum moss is useful for some plants which are grown on cork bark or for lining a hanging basket. Sharp sand is fine, washed sand, available from garden centres. Do not use coarse builders' sand. It is sometimes mixed with loam to give a specially well-drained compost.

Mixing compost: If mixing your own blend of compost, put the different items into a plastic bucket, using the same measure for each one. A plant pot or old cup will do. For 2 parts loam, 1 part peat, for example, fill the measure twice with loam, then once with peat. Mix the items together well with trowel or stick.

Lighting

Houseplants need different amounts of light, but most flowering houseplants prefer a high level of diffused daylight, but not direct sunlight. Diffused light is indirect sunlight, i.e. bouncing off a wall onto the plant or filtering through a net curtain.

Both in the northern and southern hemispheres, the sun rises in the east and sets in the west, but in the northern hemisphere in spring and autumn it shines at midday from the south, and in the southern hemisphere it shines at midday from the north. Plants placed in south-facing rooms in the northern hemisphere and in north-facing windows in the southern hemisphere, are therefore likely to receive the full rays of the sun at some time of day. Net curtains will help to shield your plant from these rays, but better still, place them well away from the window, though not in a dark corner!

Conversely south-facing rooms in the southern hemisphere, and north-facing rooms in the northern hemisphere tend to be dull and only suitable for shade-loving plants as the sun will never shine through the window.

Artificial light: To compensate for lack of daylight you can install fluorescent tubes or spotlights. However, conventional artificial light is not as intense as natural daylight and certain plants will not thrive under artificial light.

This problem occurs particularly in offices where either the windows are covered with a solar screen, or where there are no windows at all.

Special horticultural spotlights and fluorescent tubes are available which imitate diffused sunlight more closely and these have a good effect on plants. Their main drawback is that the tubes produce a very stark light and spotlights produce heat which, if focussed onto the plants, will burn their delicate leaves. For the technically minded there are other types of lamp such as mercury vapour, metal halide and low pressure sodium but for the home and office, tubes and spotlights are the most practical.

Spotlights: To imitate diffused daylight, a blue coating is added to the front of the bulb. The light seems the same as that of a conventional spotlight but in practice plants do actually grow as though they are in daylight. Unfortunately, the problem of heat has not been solved. A 150w reflector lamp mounted closer than 39in (1m) to the plant will overheat its leaves. At 39in (1m) sufficient light will be produced over an area 39in (1m) in diameter but at a distance of 78in (2m), only a quarter of that light will fall on the leaves. Although it is sometimes difficult to position the lights so as to get enough light and not too much heat, spotlights are probably the most adaptable types.

Climbers and trailers

Some flowering plants grow very fast. In a greenhouse or permanent sun porch they can be trained around the walls but in ordinary rooms they need a hoop or cane. A simple frame can be made by bending a wire coathanger or using a piece of flexible cane or plastic coated wire.

Training round a hoop

1. Push ends of wire hoop or thin cane so that they are ⅔ down pot on opposite sides. Bend stem to one side of hoop and gently twist it around the hoop. Do not damage the leaves or stem.

2. Tie a length of twine to one end of hoop and thread it along, looping it loosely around the stem. Do not tie tight knots. The growing tip will continue to follow the line of the hoop. When it reaches the other end, it can be trained round again or twisted back the other way.

Canes

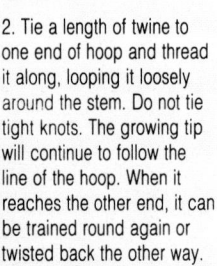

1. A single cane will support a tall plant. Insert cane when repotting, after positioning plant but before adding all the compost. Cane should be a few inches from main stem, stopping about ⅔ down pot.

A larger support can be made from two canes joined at the top by a stiff wire.

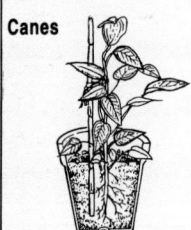

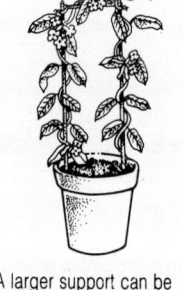

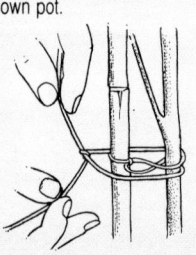

2. Loop a 9in (23cm) length of string around stem and tie in firm knot against cane. Or use a plant ring.

For three plants in one pot, place three canes around pot edge and tie at the top.

Fluorescent lights: These are a much more efficient method of providing light and are a popular source of office lighting. They do not give out much heat and are available with a wide range of intensities. Special horticultural tubes fit standard fittings and are available in the same lengths as conventional tubes. They can be used with standard tubes to give a less stark light. They are obviously not so flexible as spotlights as far as positioning goes, but if a combination of the two types is used, plants in darker areas will benefit. Most specialist plant shops will be able to advise you about what is available and give more detailed technical information.

Insecticides

Unfortunately some houseplants are vulnerable to pests and diseases. The most common are mealy bug, scale insect, red spider mite and green or whitefly. These should be treated as soon as they are noticed and affected plants moved away from others to prevent the spread of infection. Plants with thin, delicate leaves, are attacked by insects such as red spider mite while greenfly are attracted to young leaves and stems. Some pests, such as mealy bug, appear on the leaves but may be carried hidden in the soil.

Insecticides are available usually as concentrated liquids which are added to water and sprayed or watered onto the infected plant, and as aerosols ready for use. Less usually, some chemicals for houseplants come in powdered form. This is not suitable for all plants – check the individual instructions. Systemic insecticides are absorbed into the plant's veins (its system) and so spread the poison to any insect which tries to take nourishment from these.

The least toxic insecticides are those based on pyrethrum and derris as these are both natural substances. They are most suited to whitefly and greenfly control. Derris is also suitable for whitefly and greenfly and controls red spider mite in the early stages. Methylated spirits can be used to remove scale insect and mealy bugs. Red spider can be prevented from recurring by improving humidity. Malathion is one of the most effective general insecticides and will control everything from whitefly to beetles, and especially mealy bug which is one of the most infectious and damaging insects likely to affect houseplants. Other insects such as scale insect and thrips can also be controlled by spraying malathion. It can be sprayed when diluted and also watered into the soil if the soil is infected.

Malathion may damage some sensitive plants, so read the captions carefully to make sure you choose the right treatment for your plant.

Generally insecticides should be applied every 14 days until the pest disappears – but see the instructions for each plant. Fungicides, for mould and fungus infections, generally work with only one application. Check new plants for pests, as they quickly spread from plant to plant. A preventative spray in spring will guard against attack.

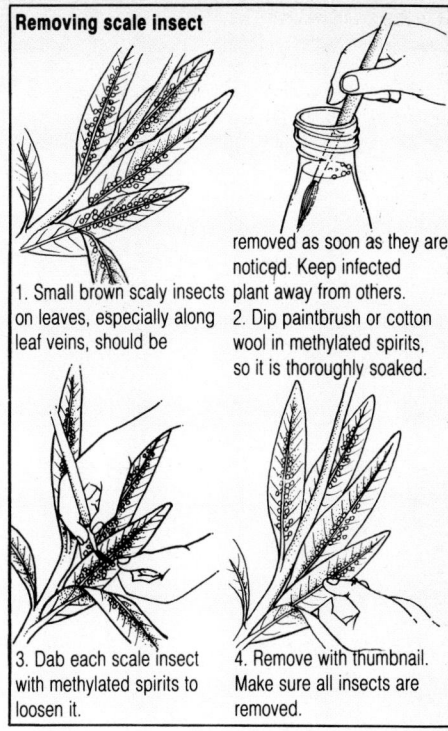

Removing scale insect

1. Small brown scaly insects on leaves, especially along leaf veins, should be removed as soon as they are noticed. Keep infected plant away from others.

2. Dip paintbrush or cotton wool in methylated spirits, so it is thoroughly soaked.

3. Dab each scale insect with methylated spirits to loosen it.

4. Remove with thumbnail. Make sure all insects are removed.

Taking care with insecticides

Insecticides and fungicides may contain deadly chemicals. Use them with care.

Never mix different types of insecticides as the chemicals may react.
Never put them into other bottles, such as soft drink or beer bottles.
Never breathe in the spray.
Never spray in windy weather.
Never pour them down the sink or drains. Do not even pour the water in which you have washed containers and sprayers down the drain.
Never make up more at one time than you will use.
Never keep diluted insecticide for more than 24 hours.
Never leave old containers lying around.
Always follow instructions carefully. Do not over or under dilute.

Always use a separate watering can and sprayer, keeping another one for normal spraying and watering.
Always keep away from food, crockery, glasses, food containers, and minerals. Derris is harmful to fish; malathion harms bees.
Always cover fish bowls when spraying.
Always store them with their sprayers and containers in a dry, frost free place, on a high shelf out of reach of children.
Always spray outside, in the evening when bees are not around.
Always wash out all sprayers and empty bottles after use, inside and out.
Always pour washing water onto ground away from food crops and water sources such as streams and rivers.
Always throw empty bottles and containers away with domestic waste.
Always wash thoroughly in hot water and detergent when you have used them.

Acalypha hispida

Chenille plant

The two varieties of *Acalypha* most popular as houseplants are quite different in appearance, though they need similar conditions to grow successfully. The Chenille plant has small green leaves and produces long, bright-red flower tassels without petals, which droop over the edge of the plant's pot. The other main type, 'Copper leaf' *(Acalypha wilkesiana)*, has heart-shaped leaves mottled red and brown.

Light: Full daylight needed, otherwise Copper leaf's colouring will not develop and the Chenille plant will not flower well. Protect from midday sun in summer.

Temperature: Winter minimum 60°F (16°C), summer maximum 80°F (27°C).

Water: 2–3 times a week in spring and early summer to keep soil moist at all times. Plant must not stand in water. When in flower, allow compost to dry out between waterings; once a week should be sufficient. In winter, once a week.

Humidity: Spray every 2 days in spring and summer until flowers start to form, then stand pot in saucer of pebbles almost covered with water to keep humidity high. In winter spray weekly, especially if in centrally heated room. Do not spray.

Feeding: Every 14 days in spring and summer, or until it ceases flowering, with liquid houseplant food diluted according to the maker's instructions.

Soil: Equal parts of peat, fibrous loam, sand, leafmould; or loam-based No. 2 with equal parts of peat and sand added.

Repotting: After a couple of years, plants begin to look straggly and it is best to take cuttings in spring and grow new plants. Cut old plants back to 12in (30cm), just above a leaf, in early spring and repot into 5in (13cm) pots with good drainage.

Cleaning: Humidity spraying sufficient. No leafshine.

Chenille plants produce striking red tassels up to 18in (46cm) long in late summer. Healthy plants should have bright green leaves and bushy side shoots growing vigorously all the way down the main stem.

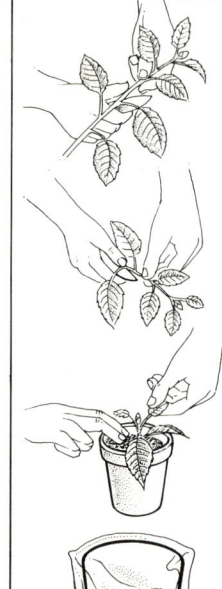
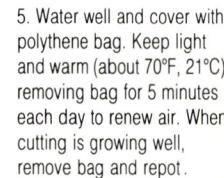

Stem-tip cuttings

1. In early spring, prepare small pot with drainage layer and compost mixed from half loam, half sand.

2. Cut off stem tip 3–4in (8–10cm) long, including growing point and at least 2 pairs of leaves. Trim off stem just below the lowest leaf.

3. Remove lowest pair of leaves. Dip cut end in hormone rooting powder.

4. Make hole in compost just deep enough to take bare stem of cutting and insert end of stem. Cut end should be at bottom of hole, lowest leaf resting on compost.

5. Water well and cover with polythene bag. Keep light and warm (about 70°F, 21°C), removing bag for 5 minutes each day to renew air. When cutting is growing well, remove bag and repot.

what goes wrong

Plant does not grow after repotting. Pot too big. 5in (13cm) pot is largest size for plant indoors.

Two-year-old plant looks straggly, long spaces between leaves. Cut back to 12in (30cm) in early spring to encourage healthy growth. Feed fortnightly in spring and summer until tassels form.

White woolly patches on leaves and stems. Mealy bug. Remove with cotton wool dipped in methylated spirits or spray every 14 days with diluted malathion until clear.

Leaves turn black. Too cold. Winter and summer minimum is 60°F (16°C). Move to warmer place. Remove black leaves.

Webs under leaves, leaves look dusty. Red spider mite. Spray every 14 days until clear with systemic insecticide particularly under leaves. Remove webs with cotton wool dipped in insecticide.

...assels do not form. Insufficient light, ...armth and food. Move to good daylight in ...mperature 60–70°F (16–21°C) and feed ...rtnightly until tassels appear.

...owers rot. Humidity too ...gh. Do not spray flowers. ...ove plant to warm place, ...out 70°F (21°C), or more ...th good air circulation.

...aves hang limply. Too ...le water in spring and ...mmer. Keep compost ...oist until tassels produced, ...en allow to dry out between ...aterings.

...aves have black patches. ...afshine damage. Do not ...e. Clean only by spraying ...th tepid water.

...althy leaves lose colour ...t light is adequate. Too ...t, plant standing in water. ...eck drainage holes in pot ...e clear. If soil stays damp ...d waterlogged even ...ugh watered infrequently, ...l mixture wrong. Repot in ...ring using correct soil.

...aves dry out. Air too dry. ...ray with tepid water every ...lays in spring and summer. ...er flowering, spray once a ...ek. Do not spray flowers.

17

Urn plant

This splendid Bromeliad grows naturally in trees with just enough roots to hold itself in place. Its out-stretched leaves gather rain into the central well, through which it absorbs the food it needs, and small quantities of methane gas which trigger flower formation. Shop-bought Urn plants usually have the flower bud formed; if not, the trigger for flowering may be provided by covering the plant after 18 months with a polythene bag for 4 weeks, enclosing a rotten apple core. After flowering, the parent plant begins to die, but new offsets form at its base.

The Urn plant's leaves have a soft, grey bloom which should never be rubbed off. It dies after flowering, so do not buy plants in full bloom. Choose one just coming into flower with healthy, unmarked leaves.

Heavy green marks on grey parts of leaves. Plant scratched, possibly by contact with domestic animal. Plant will survive as long as bloom on leaves not removed.

Light: Stands strong sunlight, survives in shade. Needs good light for flowering.

Temperature: Minimum 55°F (12°C), maximum 80°F (27°C).

Water: Fill centre well with soft water; allow excess to trickle into soil, which should be just moist. Empty well and change water every 3 weeks.

Humidity: No extra spraying necessary at normal room temperatures. Do not keep in cold, damp place.

Feeding: Not necessary but a very diluted dose of liquid houseplant food added to the water in the well every month in summer will help keep plant healthy. Use only a quarter as much food as the maker recommends.

Soil: Peat-based compost with 1 part leaf-mould or rotted pine needles to 3 parts compost. Must be lime-free.

Repotting: When plant dies, becoming dull and shrivelled, tease away offset shoots from base, carefully retaining some root. Pot up individually into 5in (13cm) pots. They will not need re-potting again.

Cleaning: Carefully with feather duster if dusty or dirty. Do not disturb grey bloom. No leafshine.

Removing the flower stem
When flower spike has died, cut its stem at base with secateurs.

Watering
Keep about 1in (2½cm) water in the plant's central well. Rainwater is best. Every 3 weeks, empty old water out and add fresh.

what goes wrong

Flower fades. Too little light. Move to better position.

Flower withers and dies. Natural after flowering.

Flower and stem rot. Soil too moist. Empty water from well and allow to dry out before watering again.

Flower and stem dry up and turn dirty pink. Too cold. Move to warmer, lighter place, at least 55°F (12°C).

Small insects in flower rosette. Blackfly. Do not spray flower. Water soil (not central well) with diluted malathion once a week for 3 weeks. Remove insects with tweezers.

...eaves shrivel. Too hot and ...ry. Move to cooler place, ...nder 80°F (27°C). Water soil ...nd ensure well in centre of ...lant is full of water.

Leaves distorted and sticky with small insects. Greenfly. Spray with pyrethrum or a systemic insecticide every 14 days until clear.

...eaves wither and die ...efore flower is dead. ...loom removed from leaves, ...r leafshine. No cure.

White woolly patches on leaves and in leaf axils. Mealy bug. Water soil (not in well) with diluted malathion. Repeat every 3 weeks if not cured.

Leaves turn brown and droop. Lime in water or soil. Use soft water for watering. Check compost is lime-free. If not, repot in lime-free mixture.

19

Anthurium scherzerianum

Flamingo flower

Though not an easy plant to grow, this is most rewarding, for the exotic flowers are long-lasting and unique in their shape and texture. Normally bright scarlet, the flowers are sometimes white, pink and, rarely, white with red markings. At the flower's centre is a long tube-like spadix which sometimes has a fascinating curl. The flowers, which appear continuously, mainly in summer, are often too heavy for their stem and may need a thin stake. They may last up to 8 weeks. With care, and knowledge of its habits, this plant should flourish.

Light: Needs plenty, but must be protected from direct sunlight.
Temperature: Winter minimum 60°F (15°C), summer maximum 85°F (29°C). Flourishes best in even temperature night and day, especially in winter.
Water: At least twice a week in summer, depending on temperature, once a week in winter, with rainwater if possible. Must never dry out.
Humidity: Spray with rainwater daily in summer, twice weekly in winter to maintain humidity. Stand pot on saucer of pebbles almost covered with water.
Feeding: Every 14 days in the growing season (spring and summer) with liquid houseplant food diluted according to the maker's instructions.
Soil: 3 parts peat-based compost to 1 part chopped sphagnum moss.
Repotting: Every other year, ensuring crown, where stems emerge from roots, is above soil level, otherwise plant may rot. If roots push up above soil level, cover them with moss.
Cleaning: Wipe leaves with damp cloth. Use leafshine every 8 weeks on leaves only.

Flamingo flowers produce their long-lasting blooms mainly in summer, but in good conditions, flowers can appear at any time of the year. Healthy plants have firm, glossy leaves and, if in flower, should have new buds appearing as well.

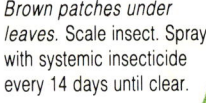

Brown patches under leaves. Scale insect. Spray with systemic insecticide every 14 days until clear.

Leaves turn yellow at tip. Too wet, overwatering. Allow plant to dry out then cut down watering by half. Check drainage holes are clear and soil mixture is correct. Plant must not stand in water.

White woolly patches under leaves and in leaf axils. Mealy bug. Remove individually with cotton wool dipped in methylated spirits or spray with diluted malathion at 10 day intervals until clear.

what goes wrong

Covering the roots
If roots at base of stem grow up through compost, cover them with moss until plant is repotted following spring.

Leaves look dull and tired. Too dark. Move to light position but not in full sun.

Brown spots on leaves. Fungus. Remove badly affected leaves. Spray plant with systemic fungicide every 14 days until clear.

Leaves dry up and become papery. Too dry. Water more often so that soil is always moist. May also be caused by dry air. If room is hot and dry, stand pot in saucer of wet pebbles and spray regularly.

Leaves droop. Too cold or in draught. Move to warmer, protected position, at least 60F (15C).

Leaves fade and become bleached. Too much direct sunlight. Move to position in good indirect light.

New leaves small and pale. Needs feeding. Increase feeding intervals to every ten days. Do not increase strength of food.

Roots push up over top of compost. Needs repotting. Repot if spring, into pot one size larger. If later in the year, cover roots with moss until following spring.

21

Ardisia

This unusual-looking flowering plant is well worth looking out for. Its oval, dark-green leaves about 2in (5cm) long, are carried round a central stem in layers or whorls. The small flowers, coloured white, red or purple, grow in clusters on stems that stick out horizontally beyond the leaves. The flowers gradually change to red berries, making the plant an attractive one to have at Christmas. Often, last year's berries may be on the plant with this year's flowers. Not difficult to keep, Ardisia forms a handsome plant up to 28in (70cm) tall, at which height it may lose its lower leaves.

Ardisia usually flowers in early summer. The flower clusters fade gradually, to be replaced by bright berries which often stay on the plant until new flower buds form the following spring. Healthy leaves are a good, shiny dark green.

Light: Best in a window out of midday sun.
Temperature: Winter minimum 45°F (8°C). Ordinary room temperature in summer. Does not mind heat, though berries stay on longer if kept under 60°F (15°C).
Water: 2–3 times a week in summer, weekly in winter. In autumn, when the flowers have all died away, leave it without water for 2–3 weeks as a resting period. Good drainage in pot essential.
Humidity: Spray 3 times a week in summer, once a week in winter. In dry air stand on saucer of pebbles almost covered with water. Don't allow pot base to touch the water.
Feeding: Every 14 days in the growing season (spring and summer) with liquid houseplant food diluted according to the maker's instructions.
Soil: Loam-based No. 2 compost.
Repotting: Annually in spring. Plant flowers and fruits best when slightly pot-bound.
Cleaning: Humidity spraying sufficient. Monthly spray with leafshine improves appearance.

Humidity
If kept in a hot, dry room, provide extra humidity by spraying at least 3 times a week.

Stand pot on saucer of pebbles almost covered with water. Do not allow pot base to touch water or roots will become waterlogged. A combination of moist soil, good drainage and humidity will keep the plant healthy in hot, dry air.

what goes wrong

Plant does not grow well in spring and no flowers appear in summer. Too dark. Move to lighter place, but not in strong midday sunlight.

Flowers drop off before fruit has set. Too cold. Move to warmer place, but not more than 60°F (15°C) if possible.

Leaves turn yellow. Too wet, overwatered or waterlogged. Check drainage holes in pot are clear and allow to dry out before watering again. In winter, water only once a week and allow to rest without water for 2–3 weeks in autumn.

White woolly patches under leaves and on stems. Mealy bug. Remove with cotton wool dipped in methylated spirits or spray with diluted malathion every 14 days until clear.

Leaves flop and go limp in summer. Needs watering. Soak plant in bucket of water for 15 minutes, then allow to drain. Water 2–3 times a week in summer, once a week in winter.

Leaves turn pale and bleached. Too much direct sun. Move into shadier place, out of midday sun.

Leaves fall off. Air too dry. Spray regularly and if temperature over 60°F (15°C) stand pot on saucer of damp pebbles. When plant is about 28in (70cm) tall, it will lose its lower leaves naturally.

Leaves mottled with sticky webs underneath. Red spider mite. Spray every 14 days with diluted malathion or systemic insecticide until clear. Spray regularly with water to keep humidity high.

23

Begonia 'fireglow'

There are literally hundreds of different Begonias, not all, of course, suitable for growing indoors. They fall into three main groups: those with fibrous roots, those with tubers (like small potatoes) and those with rhizomes (thickened underground stems).

This is a relatively new variety of the popular flowering hybrids now available nearly all year round. It is a fibrous rooted type, and is comparatively easy to keep and gives a good show of flowers. Whilst the flower colours are mostly in shades of yellow, orange and red, new varieties are being introduced, and white and pink should soon be available. Begonias like a bright, airy position, and some care must be taken in their watering.

Begonia Fireglow's bright red flowers make it one of the most popular flowering begonias. A healthy plant will look compact, with unmarked green leaves, flowers and new buds appearing, and no signs of rot on leaves or petals.

Light: Winter minimum 60°F (15°C), summer maximum 70°F (21°C). Can collapse if becomes too hot.

Water: Twice a week in summer, about every 10 days in winter. Take care if temperature drops, as overwatering can cause stem to rot. Test compost to make sure it is dry at least half way down pot. Ensure good drainage in pot. Water on leaves can cause scorching in sun.

Humidity: Spray weekly when near summer maximum. Do not get water on the flowers. Stand pot on saucer of pebbles almost covered with water.

Feeding: Every 3 weeks when in flower with liquid houseplant food diluted according to the maker's instructions.

Soil: Loam-based No. 2 compost.

Repotting: Repot once when flowering size reached. Take care as leaves are easily damaged.

Cleaning: Not necessary. Water or leafshine will damage the leaves. If dusty, use a soft, dry paintbrush – carefully.

what goes wrong

Yellow rings and mottling on leaves. Cucumber mosaic disease or tomato spotted wilt virus. No cure, destroy plant.

Brown and black patches on leaves, followed by rot. Botrytis. Too humid and stuffy. Spray with benomyl-based fungicide and move to room with drier air and good air circulation – but not draughts. Or, gas fumes. Move to fume-free room.

Leaves droop and dry up. Too hot and dry. Water and move to cooler room, less than 70°F (21°C) if possible. Remove dried leaves.

Leaves stay small and no flowers appear in spring or summer. Needs feeding. Continue feeding every 3 weeks when flowers appear, but do not feed in winter.

Repotting

1. Take care when removing soil from root ball. Begonias have delicate stems which can easily be damaged.

2. Make sure that all roots are covered with compost in new pot, but do not press it down too hard. Leave without water in shady place for 2 days after repotting.

Leaf and petal edges scorched. Too much direct sun. Move out of bright sunlight.

Spotty burn marks on leaves and flowers. Leafshine damage. Do not use.

Spots of rot on leaves, flowers and buds. Caused by spraying with water. Stop spraying.

Soft white patches on leaves. Mildew; plant probably too cold and wet. Remove affected leaves and spray with systemic fungicide. Keep in warmer, drier position.

Small blister-like spots on leaves. Leaf turns black. Bacterial wilt. Remove affected leaves and spray with systemic fungicide.

Leaves go limp and turn yellow. Too cold and wet. Allow to dry out before watering again. Move to warmer room and water only when compost feels dry below surface.

Stems rot at base. Too wet, overwatered. Allow to dry out before watering again. Move to warmer place (at least 60°F, 15°C) and water less often.

25

Bougainvillea glabra

Paper flower

Two Bougainvillea varieties are suitable for growing indoors, doing best in a sun-room or conservatory where they can be kept light and warm. They are *Bougainvillea glabra* and *B. spectabilis,* the former being the easier of the two to grow. *B. glabra* usually pruned as a bush, has mauve bracts. *B. spectabilis* is a climbing variety which includes such hybrids as 'Mrs Butt' (orange) and 'Killie Campbell' (brick red). The bracts which provide the colour look like petals but are technically special leaves. The true flowers are very small.

Light: Full daylight. Stands full sunlight, loses leaves if kept in shade.
Temperature: Winter minimum 40°F (5°C), though plant loses leaves at this temperature. To maintain leaves all year, winter minimum 65°F (18°C), summer maximum 70–75°F (21–24°C).
Water: 3 times a week in summer, once a week in winter; with tap water, as Bougainvilleas like lime. Soil must not dry out and good drainage essential.
Humidity: Spray twice weekly when flower buds appear, until flowers fade. Do not spray flowers or bracts. Stand pot in saucer of pebbles almost covered in water to maintain local humidity.
Feeding: Every 14 days in spring and summer with liquid houseplant food diluted with water. Use half as much food as the maker recommends.
Soil: Loam-based No. 3 compost.
Repotting: Annually in spring into same size pot, to change spent soil. Usual size pot for adult plant is 5–7in (13–18cm).
Cleaning: Spraying adequate – but never spray flowers or bracts. No leafshine. When not spraying, dust gently with feather duster if it looks dirty.

A healthy Bougainvillea or Paper flower has glossy, deep green leaves and, in summer, plenty of brightly coloured bracts. The actual flowers in the centre of the bracts are hardly noticeable. *Bougainvillea spectabilis* can be trained round a hoop or up a cane; *B. glabra* is usually pruned into a bush shape.

Leaves mottled yellow along veins, small scales under leaves and on stems. Scale insect. Remove with cotton wool dipped in methylated spirits or spray every 14 days with systemic insecticide until clear.

Leaves and flowers shrivel and dry, leaving coloured bracts. Too hot and dry, probably over 75°F (24°C). Water soil and spray leaves but not flowers or bracts. Move to cooler place.

what goes wrong

Leaves turn yellow and fall, webs underneath. Red spider mite. Spray with diluted malathion and water soil with same mixture once a week until clear.

Training a climbing plant
1. Push ends of wire hoop or thin cane so they are ⅔ down pot on opposite sides.

2. Bend stem to one side of hoop and gently twist it around the hoop. Do not damage the leaves or stem.

3. Tie a length of twine to one end of hoop and thread it along, looping it loosely around the stem. Do not tie tight knots.

4. The growing tip will continue to follow the line of the hoop. When it reaches the other end, it can be trained round again or twisted back the other way.

Stains and brown marks on flowers and coloured bracts. Water damage. Do not spray these. If water gets on them, shake off gently.

Growth seems stunted. Waterlogged or, if leaves also small, needs feeding. Check drainage and make sure plant is not standing in water. Allow to dry out before watering again. In spring repot into same pot with fresh compost and feed every 14 days in spring and summer, with diluted houseplant food.

White woolly patches under leaves and at leaf joints. Mealy bug. Spray with diluted malathion and water soil with same mixture once a week until clear.

No flowers or coloured bracts appear. Too dark or overwatered. Pot may also be too large. Move plant to place where it gets full sunlight and allow almost to dry out between waterings.

Scorch marks on leaves. Leafshine damage. Do not use. Clean only by spraying or with a feather duster.

Leaves fall. Natural in winter if temperature falls below 65°F (18°C). If leaves or flowers fall in spring or summer, too dark or too cold. Move to sunny place.

Leaves turn yellow. Too wet, overwatered. Allow to dry out until recovered, then water less often. Make sure pot is well drained.

Soft white patches on leaves. Mildew, caused by too damp an atmosphere. Move to more airy position, but not in draught.

Bottlebrush plant

This interesting plant originates from Australia. It needs a very light, sunny room, though it should be protected from midday sun, especially in summer. The flowers are spiked around the stem, are coloured red and yellow, and look very like a bottle-brush, hence the plant's common name. The growing shoot of leaves will push beyond the flower spike. The fruit forms below the flower, and is in the form of a woody capsule containing minute seeds which remain fertile for a long time. They are difficult to propagate but stem cuttings can be taken in early summer from young, non-flowering stems.

Light: Good, light position, shielded from direct midday sun in summer. Keep in a sunny room all the year round.

Temperature: Winter minimum 34°F (2°C) if kept dry, but best at 45–50°F (8–10°C) in winter. Ordinary room temperatures ideal in summer, but it does not like a stuffy room.

Water: Twice weekly in summer, once a week in winter, to allow top layer of compost to dry. If temperature below 45°F (8°C), keep much drier and if as low as 34°F (2°C) do not water at all. It prefers lime-free water so use soft or rainwater if possible.

Humidity: Spray once a week in summer, avoiding flowers if possible.

Feeding: Every 14 days when growing and flowering with liquid houseplant food diluted according to the maker's instructions.

Soil: 4 parts loam-based No. 2 compost with 1 part sharp sand. It prefers lime-free soil.

Repotting: Annually in spring, though plant flowers best if slightly pot-bound.

Cleaning: Humidity spraying sufficient. May be wiped with damp cloth. No leafshine.

The Bottlebrush plant grows up to 2–3ft (60–90cm) indoors and in summer produces bright red flowers near the top of its stems. The narrow leaves are greyish green in colour and a healthy plant will look bushy, with new side stems shooting in spring and summer.

Pruning
1. If plant is getting large and leggy, it can be pruned as soon as it has finished flowering.

2. Cut back stems that grew last year by up to half, making cut just above a leaf.

what goes wrong

Leaves turn yellow. Too wet, overwatered. Allow to dry out before watering again, then water less often. Check drainage holes in pot are clear.

Flowers dry up and leaves go dry and crisp. Too hot and dry. Water twice weekly in summer and if temperature 70°F (21°C) or more, spray regularly to increase humidity.

White woolly patches on leaves and at joints of stems. Mealy bug. Wipe off with cotton wool dipped in methylated spirits or spray every 14 days with diluted malathion until clear.

Flowers dry up and turn brown. Leafshine damage. Do not use.

Leaves turn very pale and look weak. Needs feeding. Feed every 14 days when producing new leaves and flowers. Use liquid houseplant food diluted with water.

Flowers fall while still in bloom. Too dark. Move to lighter place, protected from full midday sun.

Brown sticky scales on underside of leaves. Scale insect. Wipe off with cotton wool dipped in methylated spirits or spray every 14 days with diluted malathion until clear.

Leaves turn brown and fall. Too cold; frosted if plant left outside in cold weather. May not recover, but keep in warmer place, around 45–50°F (8–10°C) in winter.

Campanula isophylla

Bell flower

The Bell flower grows well as a trailing plant in a hanging basket or in an ordinary pot provided it has plenty of light and does not become too hot in summer. White, blue or mauve flowering varieties are available, the white being known as 'Star of Bethlehem'. The plant should flower throughout summer provided it is well fed during its growing season and flowers are removed as they die. In spring, plants should be cut back almost to the compost to encourage healthy new growth. Every 2 years they can then be divided.

Light: Full indirect light essential. Can take some full sun, though will dry out quickly. Keep out of very sunny windows.

Temperature: Winter minimum 43°F (7°C); best kept below 60°F (15°C) in summer, with a cooler winter rest period. Will live outside in summer but should be brought indoors in autumn.

Water: Daily in summer if on a light windowsill, to keep damp. Keep soil just moist in winter, watering every 7–10 days depending on temperature. Likes lime in tap water.

Humidity: Spray weekly in summer unless in flower. If temperature above 60°F (15°C) provide extra humidity by standing pot on saucer of pebbles almost covered in water. Pot base must not touch water.

Feeding: Every 14 days in spring and summer with houseplant food diluted according to maker's instructions. Alkaline fertilizer sticks best if available.

Soil: Loam-based No. 1 compost.

Repotting: Keep in 5in (13cm) pots and renew top inch (2½cm) soil in spring. Every 2 years, divide by removing from pot and pulling roots gently into two equal parts. Repot in clean 5in (13cm) pots with fresh compost.

Cleaning: Humidity spraying sufficient. No leafshine.

The Bell flower will produce blooms for several weeks during the summer as long as dead flowers are removed regularly. They are available in white, blue or mauve and are usually sold in flower. Choose plants with vigorous stems and plenty of new buds among the flowers.

Leaves dry, shrivel and turn yellow. Flowers die. Too dry, needs watering. Water daily in spring and summer. In winter keep soil just damp. Spray leaves weekly.

Pruning

1. Cut back straggly, woody plants in early spring, just before they are starting to grow.

2. Cut above the first pair of leaves from compost, just above the leaf joint.

3. To make an upright, bush plant, pinch out the tips from the main stems as they grow.

Stems grow lanky with long spaces between leaves and no flowers. Too hot and stuffy. Move to cooler room (below 60°F, 15°C) if possible, with better air circulation.

Leaves die off and no new ones appear in spring and summer. Too cold or needs feeding. Check temperature is between 50 and 60°F (10–15°C). Feed fortnightly in spring and summer.

Leaves and stems rot at base of plant. Waterlogged. Check not standing in water and that drainage holes in pot are clear. Allow to dry out before watering again.

Brown marks on leaves. Leafshine damage. Do not use. Clean with fine spray of water.

Rusty marks on flowers. Caused by spraying water on them. Spray leaves only.

Leaves turn black. If left outside on windowsill or balcony, frost damage. Bring indoors. Will not survive temperatures under 43°F (7°C).

Flowers rot while in bud. Too wet and too cold. Move to warmer place (between 50–60°F, 10–15°C) and allow to dry out completely before watering again. Do not spray buds.

Leaves turn yellow. Too dark, needs more daylight. Move to lighter place with some sun (not hot mid-day). Check feeding is regular in spring and summer, using fertilizer spikes if possible.

Leaves turn yellow and fall, webs underneath. Red spider mite. Spray with derris or pyrethrum or with a systemic insecticide every 14 days until clear. Do not spray flowers. Put pot on damp pebbles to improve humidity.

what goes wrong

Citrus mitis

Calamondin orange

This is a miniature orange tree which grows to a maximum height of 39in (1m). It is usually sold as a plant 2ft (60cm) high, in fruit and sometimes in flower. Its lovely, orangey scent is unmistakable. The fruits are a scaled-down version of full-size oranges, and may be candied, preserved, or used in drinks, though they are quite bitter. The plant needs a warm, light and humid position, especially at flowering time and when the fruits are ripening.

To make sure that fruits appear, spray a fine mist of tepid water on the flowers or brush each one in turn with a soft paintbrush. This transfers pollen from bloom to bloom so that fruit can form.

Light: Full light. Tolerates direct sunlight, except at midday in midsummer.
Temperature: Winter ideal 55–60°F (13–15°C); tolerates lower, but must be protected from frost. Summer maximum 65°F (18°C); good air circulation essential.
Water: Daily, with tap water, in summer. In winter allow almost to dry out between waterings. Every 7–10 days probably sufficient. Good drainage essential.
Humidity: Spray daily, early in morning. Water drops left on leaves may cause scorching in direct sun.
Feeding: Every 14 days in spring, weekly in summer, with houseplant food diluted according to the maker's instructions.
Soil: 4 parts loam-based No. 2 compost mixed with 1 part sharp sand.
Repotting: Annually in spring, taking care not to damage roots. Plants up to 2ft (60cm) happy in 5in (13cm) pots, larger plants need 7in (18cm) pots. Ensure good drainage in bottom.
Cleaning: Humidity spraying sufficient. No leafshine.

If they are to produce fruit, Calamondin oranges must be pollinated by hand. Using a camel hair paintbrush, lightly brush each flower stamen in turn so that pollen is transferred from one to another. Spray daily with tepid soft water to help fruit to set. To ripen green fruit, keep plant in a warm, sunny position.

Leaves turn quite black. Too cold. Do not allow temperature to drop below 55°F (13°C). Move to warmer place.

Leaves turn pale, then yellow. Needs feeding. Feed every 14 days in spring and summer, reducing to every 3 weeks towards end of summer. Do not feed in winter.

Plant grows leggy with long spaces between leaves. Needs pruning. Prune to neat shape in spring, cutting tops of leggy stems just above a bud, leaf or side-shoot.

Plant fails to flower. Too dark, too hot, or pot too large. Check conditions. Feed in spring to encourage new growth and do not rep again for 2 years. A 5in (13cm) pot is usually large enough.

Black dusty patches on leaves. Sooty mould. Spray with any fungicide and wipe leaves with damp cloth soaked in fungicide to prevent repeat infection.

No new growth in summer, leaves eventually turn yellow and fall. Too dark or too cold – or both. Move to warmer, lighter place (above 60°F, 15°C). Turn plant round every 3 or 4 days to make sure it grows evenly. If plant does not grow though conditions are correct, overwatering or standing in water.

Leaves turn brown and crispy. Too hot and stuffy. Move to cooler room (not more than 65°F, 18°C) if possible, with better air circulation.

Brown scales on leaves. Scale insect. Paint with cotton wool or paintbrush dipped in methylated spirits and remove with thumbnail. Spray once a month with diluted malathion until quite clear.

Scorch marks on leaves. Caused by spraying water in full sunlight. Spray in early morning or evening. Or, leafshine damage. Do not use.

what goes wrong

Leaves and buds or flowers drop. Needs watering and air too dry. Spray daily, best in early morning. Stand pot on saucer of damp pebbles. Water daily in summer with tap water but do not allow to stand in water.

Leaves turn brown at tips and curl. Too cold and draughty. Move to warmer, sheltered place, above 55°F 13°C).

Webs under leaves mottled, dusty leaf surfaces. Red spider mite. Spray under leaves with diluted systemic insecticide every 14 days until clear.

Leaves fall after turning yellow. Too wet, overwatered. Allow to dry out before watering again and make sure drainage holes in pot base are clear. In winter allow compost almost to dry out between waterings.

Leaves mottled. Leaf hopper. Spray every 14 days until clear with systemic insecticide. Water soil with same mixture diluted in water once a month to prevent another attack.

Small flies around plant. Whitefly. Spray with systemic insecticide every 14 days until clear.

White woolly patches on leaf veins. Mealy bug. Spray under leaves with diluted malathion every 14 days and water diluted malathion into soil once a week until clear.

33

Clivia miniata

Kaffir lily

This houseplant has very strong dark green leaves and, in early spring, a beautiful head of orange flowers borne on a single thick stem emerging from the centre of the leaves. The trumpet-shaped flowers usually come in a cluster of about ten blooms and are relatively long-lasting. Normally a brilliant orange, the flowers of some varieties have shades down to lemon. The plant flowers better if it is given a rest period in early winter. It slowly multiplies by making offsets as its base, so it is possible for an old plant to have several heads of flowers at a time. It is best to remove dead flowers before they produce seed. Otherwise they may not flower the following year.

Light: Stands shade, but flowers better if in a light window that does not get direct sun.
Temperature: Winter minimum while resting 45–50°F (8–10°C), increasing to 60°F (15°C) when flower buds appear. Summer maximum 70°F (21°C).
Water: Once or twice a week in spring and summer when flowering. Withhold for about a month when resting in winter.
Humidity: Stand pot on saucer of pebbles almost covered with water.
Feeding: Once a week from time flower stalk is half-grown to end of summer. Use liquid houseplant food diluted according to maker's instructions.
Soil: Loam-based No. 2 compost.
Repotting: Annually in spring after flowering for young plants, though they prefer small pots. With plants over about 3 years, change topsoil every 2–3 years and only repot when roots grow through soil at top.
Cleaning: By hand with damp cloth. No leafshine.

Kaffir lilies flower indoors in early spring, after their winter resting period. With modern commercial growing methods however, they can be made to bloom at different times of the year. The cluster of flowers ranges from orange to pale lemon yellow. Healthy plants have strong, glossy leaves, growing from a bulbous stem.

Leaves shrivel. Too dry, needs watering. Soak pot in bucket of water for 10–15 minutes, then allow to drain. Water more often, especially when flowering.

Leaves brown and scorched. Direct sun on wet leaves. Move out of strong sunlight and take care when watering not to allow water on leaves.

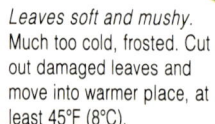

Leaves soft and mushy. Much too cold, frosted. Cut out damaged leaves and move into warmer place, at least 45°F (8°C).

Plant fails to flower in spring: Needs feeding. Feed every week when growing. If seeds were allowed to develop the year before, or plant was not given its winter rest period, it may not flower this year. If plant completely fails to grow, too cold. Move to warmer place .

New leaves pale and weak, no flowers. Too hot, air too dry. Move to cooler place, under 70°F (21°C) if possible.

Removing the flower stalk
When the flowers die, cut off stem at base before seeds begin to form.

Offsets
The small offsets that appear at plant's base can be removed to make new plants. Knock plant from pot and cut offset and its roots from parent plant with sharp knife. Repot parent and offset in separate pots.

what goes wrong

Leaves black and rotting at base. Too wet, overwatered or badly drained. Check drainage holes are clear and allow plant to dry out before watering again. Then water less often. Soil should be just moist while flowering and in summer. Leave without water for a month in winter.

White woolly patches between leaves. Mealy bug. Remove with cotton wool dipped in methylated spirits.

Cyclamen

Though winter to spring flowering is still usual, there are now cyclamen varieties which flower all year round. It can be difficult to grow, because it is very susceptible to botrytis which causes the corm, from which leaves and flowers grow, to rot. Another problem is an insect pest, cyclamen mite. When grown successfully, however, the cyclamen produces an abundance of flowers in the depth of winter. It should be bought from a reputable seller, as if it is not well cared for it may suffer damage which will not show for 2 or 3 weeks. It should not be moved around the house, as it likes to stay in one place.

Cyclamen are usually sold just coming into flower. The leaves should look firm and clean and there should be new buds appearing below the leaves. Plants may have flowers at three stages all together: small tight green buds, larger buds showing their colour and fully developed flowers.

Light: Full light essential, but shade from direct sun.

Temperature: 45–60°F (8–15°C) ideal. Likes cool, airy situation. Beware central heating, sudden temperature changes. While resting without leaves, keep cool.

Water: Twice weekly when flowering, once weekly when no flowers, from below. Increase frequency when new leaves appear, so that compost is always just moist. Never cover corm with soil or water it: it will rot. Do not stand in water or allow soil to get sodden.

Humidity: Stand on saucer of pebbles almost covered in water to maintain essential humidity. Do not spray.

Feeding: Every 14 days when growing and flowering with houseplant food diluted according to the maker's instructions.

Soil: Loam-based No. 2 compost.

Repotting: Into a fresh clay pot after flowering and when old leaves have died down. Flowers better if pot-bound, so do not use too large a pot. Leave top half of corm above soil.

Cleaning: Brush leaves gently with soft brush or cotton wool. Do not moisten or use leafshine.

Leaves turn yellow and fall apart. Too hot and dry. Water and move to cooler place.

Grey mouldy patches on leaves. Botrytis. Remove damaged leaves and spray rest with fungicide to prevent infection.

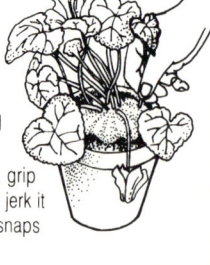

Removing old flowers and stems
When leaves and flowers die, grip each stem close to corm and jerk it upwards so that whole stem snaps off cleanly.

Plant collapses, all leaves drooping. If between waterings, needs water. If soil feels moist, caused by sudden drop in temperature, or plant too cold. Move to warmer room, but not more than 60°F (15°C).

what goes wrong

New leaves stay small, no flowers appear. Needs feeding. Feed every 14 days when new leaves start to grow.

Leaves have brown patches. Leafshine damage. Do not use.

Webs under leaves, leaves discoloured. Red spider mite. Remove affected leaves and add diluted malathion to the water when watering once a week until clear. Do not spray.

Leaves stunted and hard, dust on undersides. Cyclamen mite. No cure. Remove affected leaves and, if you have other cyclamen plants, destroy affected one.

Stems grow long and weak. Overfeeding or pot too large. Check conditions. Stop feeding until plant recovers and never give more than recommended dose of food. Repot in smaller pot after flowering.

Leaves shrivel and flop. Much too hot and dry. Wrap plant in paper so that all leaves are upright and stand pot in 2in (5cm) water for half an hour. Allow to drain and leave wrapped in paper for 24 hours in cooler room. Unwrap and continue watering normally but keep in cooler room, out of direct sun.

Stem and/or corm rots. Stem rots if corm is covered with soil. Remove surface layer to expose corm. Corm rots if it gets wet. Water always from below. Cut out rot with sharp knife and allow soil to dry right out before watering again.

Cymbidium orchid

There are about 50 species of the cymbidium orchid and modern propagation techniques have produced literally thousands of hybrids of the once rare and expensive plant, bringing it within reach of everyone. Cymbidiums are easy to cultivate though it is important to get both temperature and humidity right.

Light: Abundant light essential for regular flowering. Stands full sunlight except when in or about to flower. Benefits from being out-of-doors in summer.

Temperature: Winter minimum 45°F (8°C) if dry; otherwise 50°F (10°C) at night, 50–55°F (10–13°C) during day. In summer keep night temperatures as low as possible; up to 70–80°F (21–27°C) in the day.

Water: While growing and flowering, water 2–3 times a week to keep it moist. After flowering, reduce watering to once or twice a week for a resting period. Good drainage is essential.

Humidity: Spray every day with soft, tepid water to encourage moist atmosphere with good air circulation. Stand pot on saucer of pebbles almost covered with water to improve humidity but if colder than 45°F (8°C), remove this and do not spray.

Feeding: Weekly in the growing and flowering season with liquid houseplant food diluted according to the maker's instructions. Do not feed during the resting period after flowering until new growth starts.

Soil: 3 parts special fern (osmunda) fibre and 1 part sphagnum moss. Ready-mixed orchid mixtures are available though experienced orchid growers experiment.

Repotting: After flowering in spring if plant is pot-bound. Check roots. Usually necessary every second year.

Cleaning: Humidity spraying should keep leaves clean. If dusty, wipe with moist cloth. Do not touch flower spikes. No leafshine.

Cymbidium flowers, carried up to thirty to a stem, vary in colour from reddish brown to white. Each flower lasts for about six weeks and they open gradually along the spike. If buying plants in bloom, choose one with flower buds still to open and firm, leathery leaves.

what goes wrong

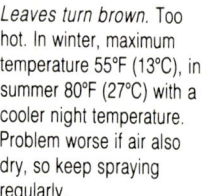

Leaves turn brown. Too hot. In winter, maximum temperature 55°F (13°C), in summer 80°F (27°C) with a cooler night temperature. Problem worse if air also dry, so keep spraying regularly.

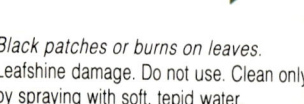

Black patches or burns on leaves. Leafshine damage. Do not use. Clean only by spraying with soft, tepid water.

Flowers have patchy, watery marks. Caused by spraying. Do not spray water or insecticide on flowers or buds.

Plant does not flower. Not enough light. Needs full light, with direct sun except when in or about to flower. When flowers appear, shade slightly to prevent scorching.

Opened flowers marked. Sun scorch. Shade from direct sun but continue to give full indirect light.

Leaves turn pale, flowers translucent. Badly drained or standing in water. Use correct compost, porous enough to allow air between the roots so that water drains rapidly away. Never stand pot in water.

Flower buds fail to open. Not enough light and needs feeding. Keep in full indirect light when flowering. Feed every week while growing and flowering.

Leaves turn black. Too cold. Minimum winter temperature 50° (10°C) unless kept dry. If dry, down to 45°F (8°C) all right for short periods.

Flower stems turn black and rot. Too humid in cold temperature. If temperature drops to 45°F (8°C) do not provide humidity.

Leaves dry out in summer. Needs watering. Soil must be always moist while growing, but plant must not stand in water. Good drainage and the correct compost are very important.

Small flies around soil surface. Whitefly, attracted by damp, humid compost. Spray with pyrethrum-based insecticide every 14 days until clear.

Cape heath

These beautiful flowering heaths are not easy to keep for long indoors as they prefer cooler winter temperatures than most people will accept. On the other hand, they will not grow outside where there is any likelihood of frost. They should be regarded as expendable, providing a little colour before winter-flowering plants such as poinsettias and azaleas become available. There are 3 varieties suitable for indoor use: pink *Erica gracilis,* white *E. nivalis* (sometimes called *E. gracilis alba),* both of which have many very small flowers, and *E. hyemalis* which has larger pink, white-tipped or yellow flowers.

Light: A window, but one that does not face direct sun ideal as plants need plenty of light.

Temperature: Winter temperature 47°F (8°C) ideal for long life. Maximum should be 60°F (15°C). Put outside in summer.

Water: 2 or 3 times a week, even in winter. Plant must never dry out, but must not stand in water.

Humidity: Spray twice weekly. Stand pot on saucer of pebbles almost covered with water or in outer pot of wet peat.

Feeding: Every 14 days when growing in spring and summer with liquid houseplant food diluted according to the maker's instructions.

Soil: 3 parts peat-based compost, with 1 part light sharp sand added. Must be lime free.

Repotting: Annually in spring after flowering. Nip out leading shoots first to keep plant bushy. Newly bought plants may be pot-bound and need immediate repotting.

Cleaning: Humidity spraying sufficient. No leafshine.

Cape heaths flower in late autumn and early winter, at a time of year when few other indoor plants are in flower. They should be kept in as cool a place as possible as they will not last long in a hot, dry atmosphere.

what goes wrong

Foliage and flowers fade and look lifeless. Too hot. Move to cooler place, under 60°F (15°C) and spray leaves with water. May also be caused by lack of light. If in dark corner, move to lighter place but not full sunlight.

Whole plant becomes brittle, leaves fall. Too dry. May be fatal but soak pot immediately in bucket of water for half an hour. Allow to drain, then water more often so that plant never dries out.

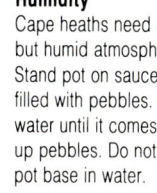

Humidity

Cape heaths need a cool but humid atmosphere. Stand pot on saucer of water filled with pebbles. Add water until it comes half way up pebbles. Do not stand pot base in water.

Another way of providing humidity is to stand the pot in an outer container, packing damp peat between the two.

Foliage and flowers darken. Too cold, probably near freezing. Move away from window at night in winter; keep above 45°F (8°C).

Irregular new growth in summer. Needs feeding. Feed every 14 days while growing. Pinch out growing tips of stems that are out of proportion.

Flowers fade. Leafshine damage. Do not use.

Brown scales on leaves and stems. Scale insect. Remove with cotton wool dipped in methylated spirits

or spray every 14 days with systemic insecticide until clear.

Leaves droop and plant smells bad. Root rot caused by bad drainage, waterlogged soil. Check plant not standing in water and that drainage holes are clear. Allow to dry out before watering again. May be fatal.

Euphorbia pulcherrima

Poinsettia

Known almost all over the world as the flower of Christmas time, today's poinsettia is an outstanding example of scientific plant breeding. It is best treated as an annual as in a warm house in late winter it soon loses its leaves unless sprayed almost daily. In cooler conditions it can be retained to flower again the following year. Its leaves, which are slightly irregular, toothed and well veined, are thin and delicate. The top leaves, nearest the small yellow flowers, are termed bracts and turn bright red; there are also pink and white varieties. If leaves or stems are damaged, a milky sap emerges which weakens the plant; it is also said to be poisonous.

Healthy Poinsettia's have bright green leaves and red, pink or white bracts below the small flowers. They need cool conditions and often drop their leaves quickly in the hot, d atmosphere of centrally heated rooms. Daily spraying will help to keep them alive and healthy from year to year.

Light: Stands direct sunlight in winter. When growing, protect from mid-day sun.
Temperature: When bracts are coloured, room temperature may be 55–70°F (12–21°C). Stands lower when growing but must be protected from frost.
Water: About twice a week unless very hot when it will dry out more quickly. Never let compost dry out when growing or in flower. After flowering, water only every 7 days for a 3–4 week rest period.
Humidity: Spray daily when in centrally-heated rooms or in summer.
Feeding: Every 14 days with liquid house-plant food while growing and flowering starts. Dilute food with water according to the maker's instructions.
Soil: Peat-based compost.
Repotting: Annually in midsummer after plant has rested. Prune stems before repotting. Handle roots and stems carefully and do not firm down compost too much. Use pot one size larger. If growing fast, repot again in autumn.
Cleaning: Humidity spraying sufficient. No leafshine.

Brown burn marks on leaves. Leafshine damage. Do not use.

Leaves look mouldy and dusty. Botrytis. Spray with fungicide every 7 days until clear.

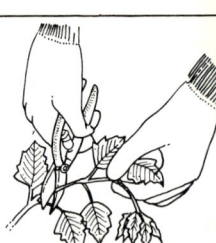

Pruning
Prune when flowers die, before repotting. Wear gloves to protect from poisonous sap. Cut stems down by half, cutting just above a leaf stem. Dust cut end with sulphur dust and if sap run seal cut with petroleum jell on cotton-wool.

what goes wrong

New leaves stay small and re pale. Needs feeding. Feed every 14 days while growing and flowering.

Leaves streaked and marbled with silver. Silver leaf virus. No cure. Burn plant.

Whole plant droops. Too cold or in a draught. Move to a protected position in a warmer room. Keep at temperature of at least 55° (12°C) when bracts are coloured. Make sure it is never exposed to frost. If too cold, plant may die.

Colour fades in patches on bracts and leaves. Too wet, overwatered, roots rotting. Allow to dry out before watering again and water less frequently in future. After flowering, allow plant to rest for 3–4 weeks, watering only once every 7 days.

Small white insects under the leaves. Whitefly. Spray every 14 days with diluted malathion until clear.

Leaves turn yellow, curl then drop. Too hot and dry.

Move to cooler place (less than 70°F, 21°C) and spray daily to increase humidity. Check soil has not dried out

Leaves turn pale and coloured bracts drop off. Too dark. Move to a lighter place. Plant will stand direct winter sunlight but protect from mid-day sun when growing.

Leaves shrivel and dry up. Too dry, needs watering. Put pot in bucket of water for 10–15 minutes, then drain. Water 50% more often. May also be affected by gas. Move to fume-free room.

Leaves distorted and sticky with green insects underneath. Greenfly. Spray every 14 days with pyrethrum or systemic insecticide until clear.

and water if it feels dry below the surface during the growing period. Keep plant out of direct sunlight. Leaves drop naturally when plant is old.

43

Gerbera jamesonii

Transvaal daisy

The flowers of this plant are very beautiful, satiny and long-lasting, compensating for rather unattractive foliage. The leaves and strong flower stems are slightly hairy and covered with a fine down. The flowers, which may be 4–5in (10–13cm) across, are available in a wide range of colours including white, peach, red, pink, mauve and magenta. Hybrid varieties are available in all these colours with a black centre. Some varieties are best suited to a frost-proof greenhouse; some improved new hybrids may be grown out-of-doors in mild areas.

Light: Good, indirect light or sunlight most suitable. Keep in light window but not in strong midsummer sun.

Temperature: Winter minimum 45° (8°C); summer maximum 65–70°F (18–21°C), with good circulation of air.

Water: 2 or 3 times a week in summer to keep compost always moist. In winter allow compost to dry out, watering only every 10–14 days.

Humidity: Spray once a week in growing season, 2 or 3 times a week when over 70°F (21°C). Do not spray in winter or when below 60°F (15°C).

Feeding: Every 14 days with liquid houseplant food diluted to half the strength recommended by the maker. Feed in spring and summer only.

Soil: 2 parts loam-based No. 2, 1 part peat, 1 part sand. Good drainage essential.

Repotting: Annually in spring into deep pots at least 6in (15cm) in diameter. Remove sideshoots, which may be taken as cuttings, when repotting. Put plenty of drainage material in bottom of pot.

Cleaning: Humidity spraying sufficient. Do not spray flowers. Do not wipe leaves, as removing hairy surface kills plant. No leafshine.

Transvaal daisies need a good, light position and will stand sun except at midday in summer. Their striking daisy-like flowers grow on a strong, slightly hairy stem and last 2–3 weeks or 1–2 weeks as cut flowers for flower arrangement

Leaves shrivel and turn brown. Either too dry or waterlogged. Check compost to see whether it is dry or wet. In summer, water every 2 or 3 days so that soil is always moist, but do not allow to stand in water. Compost must allow water to run freely through. In winter, allow compost to dry out between waterings.

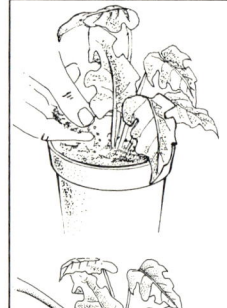

Watering

1. Always check compost before watering Transvaal daisies. In summer it should always feel moist – but not heavy and waterlogged. In winter it should feel dry and crumbly before you water it again.

2. Add water from top of pot and let it drain through into saucer. Leave for 10–15 minutes, then throw excess away. Check drainage hole in pot regularly.

Flowers do not appear, leaves elongated. Too cold and dark, needs feeding. Move to warmer place (not more than 70°F, 21°C) in good light. Will stand sunlight. Feed every two weeks with half-strength liquid houseplant food in spring and summer.

Leaves turn black. Too cold. Move to warmer room. In winter keep over 45°F (8°C) and in summer over 55°F (13°C).

what goes wrong

Plant flops. Too hot. Check temperature is not over 70°F (21°C) and move to cooler place if possible. Water and spray to increase humidity.

Black patches on leaves. Leafshine damage. Do not use. Clean only by spraying with soft, tepid water in summer. If temperature falls below 60°F (15°C) do not spray.

White fungus on leaves. Botrytis. Move to a warmer place (under 70°F, 21°C) and spray every week with systemic fungicide until clear.

Leaves rot in winter. Too wet, overwatered. In winter allow the soil to dry out at least half way down compost between waterings and do not spray if temperature below 60°F (15°C). Check soil mixture is correct and that drainage holes in pot are clear. Plant must be well drained.

Small white flies hopping around. Whitefly. Spray every 14 days with pyrethrum-based insecticide until clear.

Leaves turn brown but do not shrivel. Atmosphere too humid. May lead to botrytis. Move to warmer place, around 50°F (10°C) at least, in an airy position.

45

Hoya carnosa

Wax plant

This attractive plant would justify its place in the home just by its foliage, which is dark green, fleshy and climbs to cover a large area quite quickly. In summer, it provides the additional pleasure of waxy, star-like, flesh-coloured flowers. An established plant will be covered in blooms, have a faintly exotic aroma and produce a honey-like nectar. Moving the plant after the flower buds have set can cause them to drop off. Faded flowers should not be removed as new buds often form on them. The variegated species *H. carnosa* has attractive foliage, but is a reluctant flowerer. *H. bella* has red and white flowers. A little difficult to grow, it needs a higher winter minimum temperature, about 60° (15°C).

Wax plants have all green or variegated green and white leaves and, once well established, produce blooms of up 30 small flower heads throughout the summer months. Healthy leaves are firm and slightly fleshy and should grow all the way down the stem.

Light: Good light position, but not in mid-day sun which may scorch leaves.
Temperature: Winter minimum 50°F (10°C), summer maximum 75°F (24°C).
Water: Weekly in summer, every 14 days in winter, with rainwater if possible. Good drainage essential.
Humidity: Spray at least once a week in summer, avoiding open flowers. Stand pot on damp pebbles in outer container of damp peat.
Feeding: Every 14 days with liquid house-plant food diluted to half the strength recommended by the maker.
Soil: Loam-based No. 2 compost. Crushed brick dust in pot aids flowering.
Repotting: Plant prefers to be pot-bound, so repot only every 2–3 years into clay pots. Alternatively, simply change topsoil and feed.
Cleaning: Humidity spraying sufficient. Leaves may be wiped with damp cloth. Use leafshine not more than once a month and not on open flowers.

Training round a hoop

1. Push ends of wire hoop or thin cane so that they are ⅔ down pot on opposite sides. Bend stem to one side of hoop and gently twist it around the hoop. Do not damage the leaves or stem.

2. Tie a length of twine to one end of hoop and thread it along, looping it loosely around the stem. Do not tie tight knots. The growing tip will continue to follow the line of the hoop. When it reaches the other end, it can be trained round again or twisted back the other way.

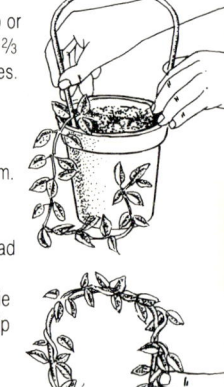

No flowers appear, leaves fade and drop. Too dark. Move to lighter place, but not in direct midday sun. May also fail to flower if pot-bound. Check roots and if they look crowded, repot in spring into pot one size larger.

Brown scorch marks on leaves. Too much direct midday sun. Or water from spraying left on leaves in bright sunlight. Keep out of midday sun and spray only in early morning.

what goes wrong

White woolly patches on leaves. Mealy bug. Remove with cotton wool dipped in methylated spirits or spray with systemic insecticide every 14 days until clear. Plant is very susceptible.

Buds drop off before opening. Too cold, too near window or plant has been moved too often. Keep above at least 50°F (10°C) in winter and do not move from place to place when flower buds have started to appear.

New leaves appear but no flowers. Needs feeding more often. Feed every 14 days all the year round with half strength liquid houseplant food. Do not increaase strength of dose.

Leaves dry up and curl. Too hot and dry. Air too dry. Keep below 75°F (24°C) and spray at least once a week in hot weather. Provide extra humidity with damp pebbles or peat. Water more often.

Brown scales on undersides of leaves, with sticky substance. Scale insect. Remove with cotton wool dipped in methylated spirits or spray every 14 days with systemic insecticide until clear.

Leaves turn yellow, wilt and rot. Too wet, over-watered. Allow to dry out before watering again and cut watering frequency by half. Good drainage is essential.

Snowball flower

Sometimes known as Hortensia, the common *Hydrangea* is well suited to growing in pots in the home and will grow happily in the garden when its flowering period is over. It needs copious watering in the flowering season or its leaves droop. It is available with pink, blue and white flowers, the latter on the beautiful 'Lace cap' variety. Pink plants may be changed to blue by adding alum (aluminium sulphate) to the soil, while blue ones may be changed to pink by adding of iron.

Light: Full light; not direct sun which dries plant out. Leaves turn yellow, growth is stunted in shade.

Temperature: Winter minimum 45°F (8°C), when dormant. Raising temperature to around 55°F (13°C) in early spring encourages growth. Summer maximum 65°F (18°C).

Water: Daily in late spring, summer, putting pot in water to cover compost for about 5 minutes or until bubbles stop rising from root-ball. Water every 2 days in early spring; only when compost appears dry in autumn, winter. Use lime-free water.

Humidity: Spray daily with soft water in spring and summer. Keep away from radiator or boiler.

Feeding: Weekly in spring and summer. Add liquid houseplant food to water in bucket, using dose recommended by maker. To avoid wasting fertilizer, drain excess back into bucket when plant fully watered and keep water/food mixture for next feed. Change mixture every 6 weeks.

Soil: Equal parts loam-based No. 2 and decayed manure, plus colourants if changing colour of flowers. Must be lime-free.

Repotting: Every year before flowering. Put plenty of drainage material in pots.

Cleaning: Humidity spraying sufficient. No leafshine.

The Hydrangea's natural flower colour is pink but can be changed to blue by adding special colourant containing alum to the water. Some soil types may produce blue flower and these can be returned to pink by adding iron filings o a colourant. A healthy plant of whatever colour should hav fresh green leaves, with no sign of drooping or discolouring.

Flowers change colour. If blue flowers turn pink, add aluminium sulphate to the water and blue colour will return. It is unlikely that pink flowers will turn blue as pink is the natural colour and is changed to blue by adding special hydrangea colouring.

Leaves turn brown and crisp. Too hot and air too dry. Move to cooler place (under 65°F, 18°C) and spray daily with soft water. Keep plant away from radiators or heaters.

what goes wrong

Young leaves distorted and sticky with green insects. Greenfly. Spray every 14 days with pyrethrum-based insecticide or diluted malathion until clear. Cut off damage leaves and keep plant away from others as greenfly sprea

Watering

Hydrangeas need plenty of water in summer and their leaves droop dramatically if the compost becomes too dry.

1. Fill bucket with water and place pot inside, with water just covering compost. Leave for 5 minutes, until bubbles stop rising from soil.

2. Remove pot and allow to drain into saucer or drip tray. Pour excess away.

3. Once a week you can add liquid houseplant food to the water. In this case, keep the water from the bucket and the excess which drains out to use another time.

oung leaves yellow, veins how up in older leaves. me damage. Use only soft ater for watering and praying and lime-free ompost. To help rapid recovery, water with sequestered iron once only.

No new growth in spring. Too cold. in early spring, move to room at least 55°F (13°C) to encourage new growth. Begin watering more frequently, every 2 days, and begin feeding every week.

Leaves turn slowly yellow and flower growth is stunted. Too dark. Move to place in good indirect light, not full sunlight.

Brown spots on leaves. Fungal infection, botrytis. Dust leaves with flowers of sulphur or spray with systemic insecticide diluted in water every 14 days until clear.

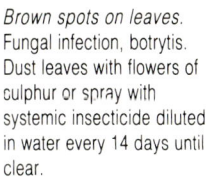

Leaves turn yellow with webs underneath. Red spider mite. Spray with diluted malathion and wipe away webs with cotton wool soaked in diluted malathion.

Whole plant is limp with drooping leaves. Eventually leaves turn brown and curl. Too dry. Plunge pot immediately into bucket of water, leave for 30 minutes then allow to drain.

Black scorch marks on leaves. Leafshine damage. Do not use. Clean by spraying with soft water.

Clog plant

The Clog plant, originally from Brazil, has curiously shaped bright orange flowers with red tips which are produced all along the plant's stems. The fleshy, bright green succulent leaves help it to conserve moisture and it can survive without water for longer than many other flowering plants. Its common name comes from the flower shape which is thought to resemble an old-fashioned clog.

Light: Good, indirect daylight, not full sunlight. Position by light window that does not face full sun is ideal.
Temperature: Never below 55°F (13°C). Tolerates summer maximum of 75°F (24°C), but good ventilation needed.
Water: Only when soil surface feels dry as too much water causes flowers to drop off. On the other hand, insufficient water also makes flowers fall. Always test compost before watering as amount needed will vary with temperature. If near summer maximum, may need water 3–4 times a week; in winter once every 7–10 days is enough.
Humidity: Likes a dry atmosphere, so no need to spray for humidity or stand pot on damp pebbles. Spraying plant when in flower rots flowers.
Feeding: Every 14 days in spring and summer with liquid houseplant food diluted according to the maker's instructions.
Soil: 4 parts peat and leaf-mould mixed with 1 part loam and 1 part sand. Or, equal parts loam-based No. 2 and peat, with a handful of sand for drainage.
Repotting: Every 2 years in spring with new compost but into same sized pot (5in, 13cm). Good drainage layer in pot essential.
Cleaning: Spray if dirty with soft water, but only when temperatures are over about 70°F (21°C). No leafshine.

The Clog plant has glossy, almost succulent leaves and pouched, orange flowers which appear all along its stems. Because its fleshy leaves help it to conserve moisture, it needs less water than other flowering plants – but do not neglect it too much or the flowers will fall.

what goes wrong

Leaf stems grow leggy with long spaces between leaves and plant fails to flower. Too dark. Move to light position but not direct sunlight. Prune plant in early spring to encourage flowering on new growth.

Pruning
Straggly Clog plants should be cut back in late spring to encourage side shoots.

Make cuts about half way up long, straggly stems, just above a leaf. Keep a neat shape.

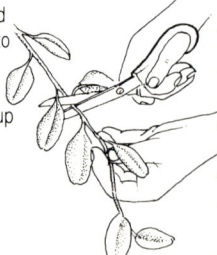

Plant does not grow in spring and no flowers form. Needs repotting in fresh soil or feeding. May be in too large a pot. Repot every 2 years in spring into 5in (13cm) pot. Feed every 14 days in spring and summer. To encourage flowering, prune plant in early spring.

Some leaves have black patches. Leafshine damage. Do not use. Clean only by spraying with soft water.

Stem tips turn brown. Too hot. Move to cooler place, under 75°F (24°C), out of direct sunlight.

White lime marks on leaves. Plant sprayed with hard water. Use only soft or rainwater for spraying and do not spray when in flower.

Leaves and flowers turn pale and some dry out though all conditions seem correct. Sunlight too strong. Move to a good light area out of direct sun. A window that does not get sun is ideal.

Leaves turn black. Too cold. Move to warmer place, at least 55°F (13°C).

Flies hopping around plant. Whitefly. Spray and water soil once a week with systemic insecticide until clear.

Webs under leaves. Red spider mite. Spray under leaves with diluted systemic insecticide every 14 days until clear. Remove webs with cotton wool soaked in same mixture.

Leaves goes soft and spongy. Too wet or atmosphere too humid. Water only about once a week in winter if temperature falls to 60°F (16°C) to allow compost in pot to dry out. In summer water when soil surface feels dry. Move to less humid place with good air circulation. May develop grey mould if in very humid, steamy atmosphere.

Flowers fall before they are finished. Either too dry or too wet. Check compost and water only when soil surface feels dry. If temperature near summer maximum (75°F, 24°C) this may be 3–4 times a week. Never allow compost to become waterlogged.

White woolly patches on leaves and at joints of stems. Mealy bug. Wipe off with cotton wool dipped in methylated spirits. Water diluted malathion into the soil every 14 days until clear.

51

Impatiens sultanii

Busy Lizzie

This is one of the easiest plants to grow indoors. It roots in water, grows very vigorously, and has brilliant coloured flowers. It can be kept from year to year, but as it tends to become leggy, sprawly and untidy, it is better either to take new cuttings each spring or to grow new plants from seed. *Impatiens sultanii* is the usual Busy Lizzie and produces plenty of pink or red flowers. New hybrids with multi-coloured foliage have been introduced. These may be treated in the same way but require slightly higher winter temperatures.

Light: Likes direct sunshine. A sunny windowsill ideal position.
Temperature: Winter minimum 55°F (13°C), though prefers 65°F (18°C). Summer maximum 72°F (22°C).
Water: 2–3 times a week in summer. Every 10 days in winter to keep on dry side, giving less if temperature drops below minimum.
Humidity: No spraying, as may cause fungus disease and mark flowers. Stand pot on saucer of wet pebbles when temperature near or over summer maximum.
Feeding: Once a week when growing in summer with houseplant food diluted in water. Use half as much food as maker recommends.
Soil: Loam-based No. 3 compost.
Repotting: Annually after first year; it flowers better when pot-bound so do not put in too large a pot. Is best to repropagate each spring.
Cleaning: Use feather duster, or put out in rain in summer, shaking surplus water off before bringing plant back inside. No leafshine.

Busy Lizzies come in all shades of pink and red, some now with reddish or variegated leaves. Healthy plants should be compact, with well-coloured leaves and, in summer, a mass of bright flowers. Old plants tend to become untidy, with straggly, fleshy stems but they are easy to propagate from either seeds or cuttings.

Spotty burn marks on leaves and flowers. Leafshine damage. Do not use. Clean with feather duster.

Leaves turn pale, stems grow long and straggly. Needs feeding or repotting. Repot in spring with fresh soil and feed once a week when growing with half-strength food.

White insects fly away when plant is touched. Whitefly. Spray with derris or pyrethrum every 14 days until clear.

Plant collapses and leaves curl. Leaves and stems start to rot. Too cold and too humid. May be fatal but allow to dry out before watering again and move to warmer place, around 65°F (18°C). Do not spray.

Cuttings

Busy Lizzie cuttings root easily in water.

1. Prepare shallow jar filled ⅔ with water, with 3–4 pieces of charcoal in bottom. Cover with foil held by rubber band and pierced with holes to take stems.

2. Remove 3in (8cm) side shoot from plant, cutting where shoot joins main stem. Push stem through foil into water. When new roots form, repot in small pot and cover with polythene for 3 or 4 days to give extra humidity.

No flowers appear. Too dark. Move into light window, in direct sun.

Plant grows straggly with no leaves on bottom stems. Too old. Take cuttings to grow new plants.

Sooty deposits on leaves. Mould from greenfly infection. Wipe off mould with cotton-wool soaked in fungicide and spray every 14 days with diluted malathion until clear.

what goes wrong

Leaves distorted and sticky with green insects. Greenfly. Spray every 14 days with derris or pyrethrum until clear.

Leaves turn pale and have webs underneath. Red spider mite. Spray with diluted malathion every 14 days until clear.

Leaves dry out, curl and die. Too hot and dry, air too dry. Move to cooler place, not more than 72°F (22°C). Water 2 or 3 times a week in summer to keep compost moist and provide humidity.

Leaves turn pale and fall off. Too cold. Move to warmer place, preferably 65°F (18°C).

White powdery mould on leaves and stems. Fungal infection. Allow to dry out and move plant to warmer place, above 55°F (13°C) at least. Spray once with systemic fungicide.

53

Mountain sage

In its natural habitat – Asia and Africa – the Mountain sage or Shrub verbena thrives as a shrub in hot, dry conditions. Indoors, it survives in normal room temperature as long as it is in good bright light, but does best of all in a sun-room or greenhouse where there is constant full light. It grows to between 2 and 4ft (60 and 120cm) tall and, to keep it compact, should be pruned in early spring each year. Its leaves are rather similar to those of the garden Viburnum. Its flowers, which appear all through the summer, range from white to violet, orange and red.

The Mountain sage's flower clusters are made up of groups of small florets, which open gradually from the outside to the centre. They change colour as they age and a single flower head may contain blooms ranging from dark red at the outside to yellow and orange towards the centre.

Light: Full light, including sunlight. Best in greenhouse or sun room, but will survive in sunny window.

Temperature: Winter minimum 55°F (13°C); constant 65°F (18°C) in summer.

Water: They grow naturally in a sandy soil. In pots, this type of soil allows water to drain through very quickly and should be thoroughly watered whenever the surface feels dry. A 5in (9cm) pot will need watering twice a week in summer and about once a week in winter at recommended temperatures. Check compost every day. Never stand pot base in water.

Humidity: Normal room humidity adequate. Do not spray. Not suitable for self-watering containers or for using in mixed bowls and troughs as soil and humidity requirements will be different.

Feeding: Weekly in spring and summer when growing with liquid houseplant food at maker's recommended strength.

Soil: 2 parts loam-based No. 2 with 1 part manure or equal parts of peat and sand.

Repotting: Annually in spring. Make sure there is good drainage in pot.

Cleaning: Dust carefully with feather duster if dirty, treating delicate flowers very gently. No spraying or leafshine.

Plant grows straggly. Needs pruning to encourage flowers and bushy growth. Prune in late winter.

Pruning

To keep them compact and to make sure of continued flowering, plants over 2 or 3 years old should be pruned in early spring.

1. Cut stems back to about 6in (16cm) above compost, just above a leaf.

2. When flower heads die, cut them off cleanly at point where flower stalk joins main stem.

White fungus on leaves. Botrytis. Caused by too much humidity. Move to better ventilated place and water soil with systemic fungicide every week until clear. Do not spray fungicide as this will damage leaves.

Leaves have black patches. Leafshine damage. Do not use. Do not spray leaves with water either. If dirty, brush lightly with feather duster.

Leaves have blotchy brown patches. Too much humidity. Move to drier, more airy atmosphere and do not spray with water.

Plant does not flower in summer. Too dark and/or too cold. Keep at constant 65°F (18°C) in summer in full light, including sunlight. Move to a sunny window.

Flies hopping around plant. Whitefly, aggravated by too much humidity. Add systemic insecticide to the water every 14 days until flies disappear. Place plant in more airy place.

Leaves droop and turn brown. Needs water. Plant has been left for too long between waterings. Water immediately and then water more regularly.

Plant does not produce new leaves or stems in spring or summer. Soil exhausted. Repot in spring or autumn with good drainage in the pot. In summer, add liquid houseplant food to the water every week.

Leaves turn black. Too cold. Needs a temperature of at least 55°F (13°C) in winter and 65°F (18°C) in summer.

Leaves wilt and droop. Too wet, overwatered or waterlogged. Allow to dry out before watering again and in future water only when soil surface has dried out. If plant wilts though watering is correct, too hot. Move to cooler place, under 65°F (18°C) if possible.

what goes wrong

Medinilla magnifica

Rose grape

This beautiful tropical plant, though expensive to buy, is very rewarding. Its exquisite flowers, enhanced by wide pink bracts and hanging flower stems, continue for long periods in perfect condition and will appear year after year, providing conditions are right and the soil is changed frequently. Since a humid atmosphere is essential for successful growth, the plant does best in a heated greenhouse, sun-room or conservatory.

Light: Full daylight but shaded from direct sun.

Temperature: Winter minimum 60°F (15°C); summer maximum 75°F (24°C); in autumn around 70°F (21°C).

Water: 2–3 times a week in spring and summer to keep soil moist at all times. Allow compost to dry out between waterings in winter; once every week to 10 days enough. Never stand pot in water.

Humidity: In the house, stand pot on saucer of pebbles almost covered in water to provide local humidity and spray daily with tepid soft water in spring, until flowers appear. Then spray once or twice a week and put plant in more airy place. After flowering remove saucer of damp pebbles and spray only once a week.

Feeding: Weekly in spring and summer with liquid houseplant food at maker's recommended strength. After flowering, stop feeding until following early spring.

Soil: Equal parts of decayed leaf-mould, good fibrous loam with a sixth part of silver sand and a few grains of charcoal.

Repotting: Annually in spring into pot one size larger for young plants. Ensure good drainage in pot. When plant reaches its maximum indoor height (about 4ft, 120cm) just replace compost and leave in same sized pot.

Cleaning: Clean leaves with tepid soft water. No leafshine.

The Rose grape is one of the most beautiful tropical plants grown indoors, producing spectacular hanging pink flowers on the ends of 18in (50cm) stems. The leaves are leathery and grow direct from the stems. These may become woody in time but the plant can be kept compact and vigorous by regular pruning.

After flowering

1. As flowers die, cut them off above the first leaf with a sharp knife. The plant's energy will then be transferred to the new buds.

2. When all flowers are dead and there is no sign of new buds, prune plant to keep it in good shape and encourage development of strong new shoots. Use a sharp knife and cut just above a leaf, cutting stems back by half. Dust cut end with sulphur dust.

Leaves droop, turn yellow and fall. Soil feels moist. Plant waterlogged, roots rotting. Do not stand plant in water and check that drainage holes in pot are clear. Allow to dry out before watering again.

Plant does not grow in spring or flowers do not form. Pot too small or needs feeding. Repot in spring with fresh compost even if keeping plant in same size pot. Feed weekly in spring and summer.

what goes wrong

Webs under leaves, underside of leaf dusty. Red spider mite. Very common. Spray with quarter strength systemic insecticide once a week until clear. Spray with soft water on sunny days, especially under leaves, to improve humidity.

Leaves turn pale and no flowers appear. Too dark. move to good, light position.

Leaves have brown patches. Air too dry. Spray daily with tepid soft water in spring until flowers appear.

Leaves turn black. Too cold. Do not allow winter temperature to fall below 60°F (15°C). In summer, best around 70°F (21°C).

Bracts turn transparent. Too much humidity. When flowering, do not spray every day and put plant in airy position.

Flower buds do not develop into flowers. Needs feeding. Feed every week in spring and summer while flowering. Remove old and faded flowers as they die off.

Tips of leaves turn brown, flowers marked. Too much direct sunlight. Move into good light, out of bright sun. Round spots are caused by spraying with water in strong sunlight.

Small flies hopping around plant. Whitefly. Spray plant with quarter strength insecticide every 14 days until clear. If in greenhouse, fumigate with smoke bomb.

Leaves have black patches. Leafshine damage. Do not use. To clean, spray only with tepid soft water.

Leaves droop. Too dry. In spring and summer, water daily to keep soil always moist but do not allow to stand in water. If plant droops though soil is moist, too hot. Try to keep plant at not more than 70°F (21°C) in summer.

57

Neoregelia carolinae tricolor

Cartwheel plant

This striking plant has long, strap-like green and cream leaves with, in the centre, a group of special leaves or bracts which turn a rich red. The actual flowers are small, usually mauve in colour, and hardly project out above the central leaves. It is a Bromeliad, one of a large famiiy of plants which includes the Pineapple. Many of them grow in trees in their natural habitats and absorb nourishment from water that collects in their central well rather than from soil. The Cartwheel plant's leaves spread out almost horizontally and span up to 18in (46cm). A recently introduced more compact variety, 'Perfecta', has an intense red colour. There is also a widely grown plain green variety, 'Marechalli'. All make useful plants for mixed groups in large tubs or troughs.

Light: Good light position with some sun. Avoid midday sun.

Temperature: Constant all-year 60°F (15°C) ideal. Acceptable winter minimum is 55°F (13°C), summer maximum 70°F (21°C).

Water: Keep rosette centre half full with water at all times, changing the water weekly. Water compost weekly in summer, keep drier in winter, watering every 10–14 days.

Humidity: Spray overhead weekly.

Feeding: In summer, add liquid houseplant food when changing water in central well every second week. Use half as much food as the maker recommends.

Soil: Equal parts peat-based and loam-based No. 2 compost.

Repotting: Annually in early summer. Roots are small but plant may need bigger pot for support since leaves tend to spread out.

Cleaning: Wipe leaves with damp cloth. No leafshine.

The Cartwheel plant's tiny flowers grow inside its central well and it is the brightly coloured bracts that are its most striking feature. The plant flowers only once so when buying make sure that there are no signs of old flowers and that the striped outer leaves are clean and undamaged.

Leaves droop, dry out and look pale though watering correct. Too hot. Keep below 70°F (21°C), constant 60°F (15°C) ideal.

Leaves look bleached. Too much strong midday sun. Move out of direct summer sun but keep in good light.

what goes wrong

Plant dries up and shrivels. Too dry. Make sure that there is always water in the plant's well and that the soil in pot is watered regularly.

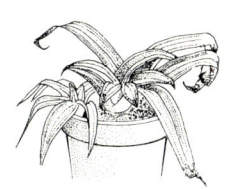

Removing offsets

When flowers and leaves of parent plant have quite died down, offset will be about half the size of parent and will be ready to separate.

1. Prepare small pot with drainage layer and mixture of damp peat and sand.

2. Knock plant from pot and cut offset and its roots from old plant with a sharp knife.

3. Place offset in new pot and firm compost around its base, covering roots. Water well and cover pot with polythene for 2–3 days to provide extra humidity. Discard parent plant.

Leaves turn pale. Too dark. Move into lighter place, with some direct sun, but not at midday in summer.

Leaves fade and have webs underneath. Red spider mite. Spray every 14 days with diluted malathion or derris.

Centre of rosette starts to die but young side shoots appear. Natural after 2–3 years. Do not separate new shoots until centre of parent plant has died.

Flowers shrivel and turn black. Leafshine damage. Do not use on flowers.

Base of plant rots. Too cold and wet. May be fatal, but allow to dry out and empty water from central well until plant recovers.

Brown scales under leaves. Scale insect. Remove with cotton-wool dipped in methylated spirits or spray with systemic insecticide every 14 days until clear.

Oleander

The oleander is a pretty plant with soft-coloured trumpet-shaped flowers in both double and single form. The leaves are long and narrow and paired down the stem. Its foliage and, in some circumstances, flowers are poisonous and should never be eaten by humans or animals. Oleanders grow up to about 18in (46cm) in a pot though in a large tub in a conservatory or sun-room they may reach over 7ft (2m). The variegated types, *Nerium oleander* 'Variegata', tend to be more compact and slower growers. Flower colours range from white through delicate pink to orange and even purple. Some are scented. After flowering, the stems which have carried flowers can be cut back to half their length. Use secateurs and cut at an angle just above a side shoot or leaf.

Oleander flowers come out in succession all through the summer, although each one lasts only a short time. Healthy leaves are naturally slightly matt and leathery. When buying, choose a plant with buds as well as flowers and check leaves for signs of pests.

Light: Very light position, does not mind full sun. Too much shade prevents flowers from appearing.

Temperature: Winter minimum 40°F (5°C). Prefers to be cool in summer; if over 60°F (15°C) must be outside or in a very airy room.

Water: Daily in summer if over about 65°F (18°C) every 10 days in winter, using tepid rainwater if possible. If water is cold, flowers may not form.

Humidity: Spray with soft water once a week in summer, especially if over 65°F (18°C), but never in middle of day.

Feeding: Every seven days in summer when growing, using liquid houseplant food diluted according to maker's instructions.

Soil: Loam-based No. 3 compost.

Repotting: Usually every 2–3 years in spring. Plant flourishes in big pot. When not repotting, change topsoil in spring and feed.

Cleaning: Spray with tepid water or wipe with damp cloth if dirty. No leafshine.

Side shoots

1. To encourage buds to open, cut off side shoot immediately below flowering head so that plant's energy all goes to buds.

2. Put stems into shallow jar filled ⅔ with tepid water and covered with foil. 3 or 4 pieces of charcoal will keep water fresh. If kept warm (61–64°F, 16–18°C), new roots will form and cuttings can then be potted in small pots. Cover them with polythene for 2–3 days to give them extra humidity.

Leaves pale with no new growth. Needs feeding or repotting. Repot every 2 to 3 years in spring and change topsoil in other years. Feed weekly in summer.

Buds rot before opening. Too cold, or water too cold. Move to warmer position (not over 60°F, 15°C if possible unless in very airy room) and water with tepid water in winter.

Leaves pale, dry and shrivelled with no new growth. Too dry. Soak pot in bucket of water for 15 minutes, then drain. Water daily in summer to keep moist.

Stems grow straggly with no flower buds in summer. Too hot and dry. Water daily in summer and spray with soft water. Move to cooler place (under 60°F, 15°C if possible) or very airy room.

what goes wrong

Brown marks on leaves. Too cold, if plant outside may be frost 'burns'. Winter minimum temperature 40°F (5°C). Brown marks on flowers may be caused by leafshine. Do not use.

Scorch marks on leaves. Caused by water staying on leaves in strong sunlight. Spray only in early morning and make sure water does not stay on leaves.

White woolly patches on leaves and in leaf axils. Mealy bug. Remove with cotton-wool dipped in methylated spirits or spray every 7 days with systemic insecticide until clear.

No flower buds appear but leaves and stems otherwise healthy. Too dark. Move to lighter position, in full sun.

Brown scales under leaves and on stems. Scale insect. Remove with cotton-wool dipped in methylated spirits or spray every 7 days with systemic insecticide until clear.

61

Pachystachis lutea

Lollipop plant

A relatively recent introduction to the realm of flowering houseplants, the Lollipop plant is not unlike the more common 'Shrimp plant', *Beloperone guttata*. Both belong to the same family of Acanthaceae. The bright yellow bracts of the Lollipop plant stand upright at the top of the leaf-stems. Between the bracts are small white, snap-dragon-like flowers. The plant may be grown for its foliage when flowering is over, though it should be pruned back by half after flowering to keep it compact.

The Lollipop plant's yellow spikes are formed of special leaves or bracts; the true flowers are the small white petals which grow from the sides. A healthy plant will have firm, bright leaves all the way down the stems. If they are pale, dull or droopy, the plant needs care and attention.

Light: Full light, including summer sun. Prefers shadier position in winter when dormant.

Temperature: Summer average 60°F (15°C) preferred, with maximum 70°F (21°C). Lower in winter, though if as cool as 45°F (7°C) plant will temporarily lose leaves.

Water: In summer keep compost always moist, watering 2–3 times a week, more often if it dries out more quickly in hot weather. In winter water about once a week. Compost should never dry out completely, but do not allow to become water-logged. Do not stand in water.

Humidity: Spray 2 or 3 times a week and stand pot on saucer of damp pebbles to give extra humidity. Do not spray when bracts are forming as they will rot.

Feeding: Weekly in growing season with liquid houseplant food diluted according to the maker's instructions.

Soil: Loam-based No. 2 compost. Good drainage essential.

Repotting: Annually in early spring. A 5in (13cm) pot adequate for plants up to 5 years old. Put plenty of broken crocks or pebbles in pot to improve drainage.

Cleaning: Gently dust with soft brush or feather duster if dirty. No leafshine.

Plant grows straggly, with long spaces between leaves. Needs pruning. Prune in early spring to encourage a bushy plant with many flowers.

Pruning
When flowers and bracts have died, cut the stems back severely to within 3–6in (7–15cm) of compost. Cut just above a leaf stem.

Humidity
Stand pot on saucer of pebbles almost covered in water to provide extra humidity but do not let base of pot stand in water, as compost must be well drained. Do not spray when bracts are forming or they will rot.

what goes wrong

Flowers and coloured bracts rot and drop off. Plant in stuffy room, or flowers and buds have been sprayed with water. Move to airy but not draughty place and stand pot on damp pebbles.

Plant does not grow in spring and summer. Too dark and/or needs feeding. Needs full light in summer, including sunlight. Feed weekly in spring and summer.

White woolly patches under leaves and in leaf joints. Mealy bug. Remove with cotton-wool dipped in methylated spirits. Water soil every 6 weeks with diluted malathion.

Small flies hopping around plant. Whitefly. Spray underside of leaves and soil every 14 days until clear with pyrethrum-based insecticide.

Leaves turn pale and lose gloss. Needs feeding or repotting. Repot in spring with fresh compost and feed every week in growing season, especially when flowering.

Leaves flop then drop. Too dry, roots dried out. Soak pot in bucket of water for 30 minutes, then allow to drain. Water more frequently, so that compost is always moist.

Leaves mottled yellow, especially along the veins. If brown scales on leaves, scale insect. If leaves sticky with small insects, greenfly. Remove scale insects with cotton-wool dipped in methylated spirits. For both pests, water soil with diluted systemic insecticide once a week until clear.

Leaves dry out and turn crisp. Too hot, air too dry. Keep below 70°F (21°C) if possible and place pot on saucer of damp pebbles to increase humidity. Do not spray.

Leaves distorted and sticky with green insects. Greenfly. Spray underside of leaves with pyrethrum-based insecticide every 14 days until clear and water diluted systemic insecticide into the soil every 14 days. Move to a more airy position.

Leaves become dull and droop, lower leaves fall. Too cold and/or roots waterlogged. Plant needs temperature of at least 60°F (15°C) in growing period. Never allow to stand in water though compost should be moist. If compost feels heavy and wet, allow surface to dry out before watering again. Check drainage holes in pot are clear.

Leaves fall in winter. Too cold. Move to warmer place, about 50°F (10°C).

Regal pelargonium

Pelargoniums are often confused with geraniums, outdoor garden plants to which they are closely related. The varieties grown indoors as houseplants are real sun-worshippers and require the protection of a sun-facing window. They are most satisfying, colourful plants to grow in summer, and are not difficult providing they are in good light, airy positions and are well watered.

Pelargoniums have large heads of flowers, delicately coloured from the softest of pinks to the darkest of reds, often with a contrasting deeper shaded area in the middle of petals. When the flower-heads have died, break them off at the point where they join the main stem. In spring a straggly plant can be pruned back to about half its size.

Light: Sun-facing window essential to provide sufficient light all year round.

Temperature: Winter, 55–60°F (13–15°C); summer, ordinary room temperature to maximum 75°F (24°C).

Water: 2–3 times a week in summer, with good drainage in pot. About once every 10 days in winter to keep on dry side. If below 60°F (16°C), withhold water.

Humidity: Fairly dry atmosphere preferred. No overhead spraying, as this can produce stem rot. Do not stand pot on damp pebbles.

Feeding: Every 14 days in spring and summer when growing with liquid houseplant food diluted according to maker's instructions.

Soil: Peat-based or loam-based No. 1 compost.

Repotting: Twice during first year. After this, since plant flowers better if pot-bound, change topsoil each spring and feed.

Cleaning: Use feather duster if very dusty. Do not spray. No leafshine.

Healthy Pelargoniums have clean-looking green leaves, w no sign of yellowing or damaged edges. In a sunny windo they produce a succession of buds from late spring to the end of summer, opening into bright clusters of flowers rangi in colour from pale pink to deep red.

Plant grows straggly, with long spaces between leaves. Bottom leaves turn yellow. Too dark. Move into light window, facing the sun.

what goes wrong

White insects fly away from plant when touched. Whitefly. Spray with derris or pyrethrum-based insecticide every 14 da until clear.

Mass of distorted shoots at soil level. Leafy gall, a bacterial disease. Destroy plant and do not use as cuttings. No cur

Lots of healthy leaves grow but no flowers. Overfeeding. Feed only every 3 weeks instead of every 14 days and never exceed recommended strength of dose. Try changing the brand of houseplant food.

Watering

1. Pelargoniums need careful watering to keep them moist but not waterlogged in summer, drier in winter. Always test compost surface before adding water.

2. Water from top of pot and allow excess to drain through. After 10 minutes empty away any that remains in the saucer. If temperature falls below 60°F (16°C) do not water.

Leaves turn yellow and have brown blotches. Too dry and stuffy. Water more often, 2 to 3 times a week in summer and move to more airy position.

Leaves darken and develop a red tinge. Too cold at night. Move to warmer place and do not allow temperature to fall below 55°F (13°C).

Pale yellow rings on distorted leaves. Virus disease. No cure. Destroy plant.

Bottom of stem turns black and rots. Fungal disease called black leg. Caused by cold and overwatering. Usually fatal but move plant to warmer room (around 60°F, 15°C) in winter and allow plant to dry out before watering again.

65

Miniature rose

Miniature roses are the only type that grow successfully as houseplants. Growing to 9–12in (23–30cm) high, they produce single, double or clusters of flowers, according to the variety. Their main requirements are good light and high humidity during the growing period in spring and summer. Once the flowers are over, the pots should be taken outside and sunk to their rims in soil; a layer of moist peat should be added to the top of the compost and they should be fed with fertilizer diluted to half normal recommended strength. If this is not possible, keep them in as cool a place as possible after flowering, to give them a 2 month dormant period. In early spring, prune away half the new growth from the previous year, cutting with scissors or secateurs just above a new bud.

Miniature rose bushes, up to 12in (30cm) high, make unusual indoor plants and, provided they can be kept in light, humid conditions, produce flowers every two months throughout the year. In drier conditions they should be put outside after flowering in summer and brought back indoors when a new crop of buds appears.

Light: Full daylight, including sun.
Temperature: Winter indoors at 45°F (7°C), or outdoors (see above). In early spring gradually increase temperature as growth begins. Summer maximum 70°F (21°C).
Water: 2–3 times weekly in summer, once a week in winter, just enough to stop compost from drying right out.
Humidity: Spray daily in spring and summer, avoiding flowers, especially in strong sun, as droplets may burn plant. Stand pot on saucer of damp pebbles.
Feeding: Every 14 days in spring and summer when growing with liquid houseplant food at maker's recommended strength.
Soil: Equal parts of loam-based No. 2 and peat-based composts.
Repotting: Annually in early spring into next size pot. They flower best if pot-bound, so do not use too large a pot.
Cleaning: Humidity spraying sufficient. No leafshine.

White powdery mould on leaves and buds. Mildew. Caused by dry roots, poor feeding and hot days followed by cold nights. Spray immediately with fungicide and repeat weekly until clear.

Black powdery mould on younger stems. Sooty mould. This forms on sticky substance left by greenfly. Spray twice weekly with diluted malathion and fungicide until clear.

Centre of leaves pale. Magnesium shortage. Use special rose fertiliser containing magnesium. Some tomato fertilisers are suitable – check contents on label.
Young leaves pale green with red spots. Nitrogen shortage. Feed every 14 days with liquid houseplant food in spring and summer and use correct compost.

what goes wrong

Plant grows straggly with no flowers. Too dark. Move into light window where it will get full sun.

Plant wilts, though leaves do not fall. Needs water. Water 2–3 times a week in summer, once a week in winter but do not allow to stand in water.

Green insects covering buds and flower stems. Greenfly. Spray every week with systemic insecticide until clear. Water same mixture into soil once a week until clear.

Leaf veins turn pale yellow or cream. A harmless virus disease. Needs feeding.

Leaves have large yellow patches. Too much lime in soil. Use a standard rose fertiliser every two weeks in spring and summer. If problem persists, apply one dose of sequestered iron.

Leaves turn brown and crisp. Too hot and air too dry. Summer indoor maximum temperature 70°F (21°C). Spray daily in spring and summer – though not in bright sunshine. Stand pot on damp pebbles to provide extra humidity.

Flower petals eaten. Thrips. Very common in hot summer on indoor plants. Spray every week with diluted malathion until clear.

Black burn patches on leaves. Leafshine damage. Do not use. Clean only by spraying with soft water.

Veins turn yellow, leaves develop large yellow areas. Waterlogged. Never stand plant in water. And allow surface soil to become dry between waterings.

Leaves crinkled with brown marks. Frost damage while overwintering. If outside in long, frosty periods, cover plants with straw and wrap in sacking.

Leaves have large black spots surrounded with yellow. Leaves fall. Black spot. If not treated, all leaves will fall and plant will die. Spray twice a week with fungicide and improve air circulation around plant. Remove and burn affected leaves and stems.

Gloxinia

One of the most beautiful of summer plants, the Gloxinia can, with a little care and attention, be kept going for more than a season. The size and quality of its blooms deteriorate after two or three years, when it may be better to start again. It is also difficult to transport as its wide, flat leaves crack and break easily. The plant's trumpet-shaped flowers are carried singly on stems about 8in (20cm) above the leaves. They are available in many colours, including red, white, mauve, pink and multi-colours.

Light: Good light position, avoiding direct mid-day sun.

Temperature: 60–70°F (15–21°C) summer indoors. Plants should die down in autumn, and the tubers be stored in a dry place, minimum temperature 40°F (6°C). Move to temperature of 70°F (21°C) in early spring to start new growth.

Water: 3 times a week in summer, reducing in autumn until completely dried off. Water must not go on crown (centre) of plant.

Humidity: Mist spray every day with tepid water when growing, avoiding flowers. Shake surplus off leaves. Provide local humidity by standing pot on saucer of pebbles almost covered with water or in outer container with damp peat.

Feeding: Weekly when growing in spring and summer with liquid houseplant food diluted according to the maker's instructions.

Repotting: 2–3 times in first year for young plants grown from seed or cuttings. Repot old tubers each year in fresh compost when winter rest period is over. Use same sized pot as before, allowing tuber to fit comfortably across width of pot. Half bury tubers in compost, leaving top exposed.

Cleaning: Humidity spraying sufficient. No leafshine.

Gloxinias have velvety, trumpet-shaped flowers and wide leaves with distinct vein markings. As the first flower opens there should be many new buds growing at its base. The dark green rather fleshy leaves should be firm and undamaged, with no curled or discoloured edges.

what goes wrong

Leaves cracked or split. Plant has been knocked or damaged while moving. Be careful of plants fragile leaves.

Leaves distorted and sticky with green insects. Greenfly. Spray with pyrethrum or systemic insecticide every 14 days until clear.

Repotting

1. Repot tubers in early spring, just before new growth starts. Prepare pot same size as before, wide enough for tuber to fit easily with at least 1½in (3cm) space around it for stems and shoots to grow. Put good drainage layer in bottom and layer of peat-based compost ⅔ way up pot.

2. Place tuber on compost and add more until it is half buried. Do not cover it completely, but firm compost around it so that roots are well covered.

3. Leave without water for 2–3 days then water and bring into warmer room (70°F, 21°C) to encourage shoots to appear. Water once or twice a week.

4. When shoots are growing well, increase watering to 2 or 3 times a week, so that compost is always moist but not waterlogged.

Leaves and buds rot. Too cold and/or water on crown of plant. Move to warmer place (at least 60°F, 15°C) and allow soil around crown to dry out before watering again. Water from below, not top of soil. In winter, allow soil to dry out completely.

Brown rings on leaves. Tomato spotted wilt virus. No cure, destroy plant immediately. Or leafshine damage. Do not use.

Flowers marked and stained. Caused by spraying flowers with water. Do not spray or if water gets on to them, shake it off immediately.

New leaves small and pale. Needs feeding. Feed every week in spring and summer with liquid houseplant food.

Small flowers on short stems. Too dark. Move to lighter position, in window but out of direct midday sun.

Leaves curl and go limp. Too sunny and too dry. Water (from below) and move out of direct sun.

69

Solanum capsicastrum

Winter cherry

The Winter cherry is one of 900 plant species in a family which includes the potato. It produces flowers in summer, followed in autumn by attractive berries which remain on the plant through the winter and even into early spring. Although not poisonous, they should not be eaten as they can cause a violent stomach upset. Winter cherries must not be kept in too warm a position; outside they will grow in window-boxes in winter, provided they are kept frost free. After the berries have fallen, the plants should be cut back to half their original size. Cut each stem just above a leaf. In autumn, pinch out tips of non-flowering stems.

Light: Full light, including direct sunlight. Cool but sunny window ideal.
Temperature: Winter minimum 40°F (5°C), though 55°F (13°C) ideal. Summer maximum 65°F (18°C), especially inside.
Water: 2–3 times a week in spring and summer so that plant never dries out. Once every 14 days in winter to keep just moist.
Humidity: Spray daily in summer with soft water in early morning. Stand pot in saucer of pebbles almost covered with water but do not allow pot base to touch water. Or put pot in outer container or trough of damp peat.
Feeding: Weekly in spring and summer with liquid houseplant food diluted according to maker's instructions.
Soil: 3 parts loam-based No. 2 with 1 part peat.
Repotting: Annually in spring, with gravel in pot for drainage. 5in (13cm) pot adequate for adult plant.
Cleaning: Humidity spraying sufficient. No leafshine.

The Winter cherry's tiny white flowers appear in midsummer and are followed by a crop of berry-like fruits which change colour slowly from green to bright orange-red. These stay on the plant all through the winter as long as it is kept in a cool but humid position.

No berries form after flowering. Flowers not pollinated. Spray flowers with tepid soft water or brush each in turn with soft paint brush to transfer pollen.

what goes wrong

Plant stunted with yellow rings on leaves. Tomato spotted wilt virus. No cure. Burn plant.

Plant has few leaves. Too dark. Move into cool but sunny window. Needs full light to grow well.

Berries shrivel, new leaves dry up. Too hot. Move to cooler place, under 65°F (18°C) in summer, in winter 55°F (13°C).

New leaves have furry patches. Botrytis caused by too much humidity in a cool temperature. Spray with fungicide at first signs. Move to warmer, less humid place.

Some leaves develop black patches and shrivel up. Leafshine damage. Do not use. Spray only with soft water.

Leaves turn yellow though soil feels damp. Air too dry. Spray weekly with soft water but not when plant is in bright sunshine or sun will burn leaves.

Leaves turn pale. Needs repotting or feeding. If early spring, repot in fresh compost. If in spring or summer feed every week with liquid houseplant food.

All leaves turn black and berries shrivel. Too cold. Frost damage. Move to frost free place and cut away damaged leaves and stems. Plant may recover in the spring.

Leaves have webs underneath and then turn yellow. Red spider mite. Spray every 14 days with diluted malathion until clear.

Some lower leaves turn yellow with brown spots. Magnesium deficiency. Feed once a month with tomato fertiliser instead of usual liquid houseplant food.

Leaves droop, bottom leaves and berries drop off. Too dry. Soak pot in bucket of water until bubbles stop rising. Never allow plant to dry out, especially in spring and summer.

Plant does not grow though all conditions are correct. May be waterlogged (plant must never stand in water) or in too large a pot. Check drainage holes are clear and size of pot. A 5in (13cm) pot is adequate for a full grown plant.

71

Spathiphyllum wallisii

Sail plant

This is a good dual-purpose plant for its leaves are attractive and it has graceful white flowers which are long-lasting and almost continuous from the time the plant is about 6 months old. The flowers are carried on a long stem, the outer part (the spathe) is white and the central spadix cream; with age they both turn a delicate green. When each flower withers, cut its stem off with scissors or secateurs, close to the compost. Dead leaves should also be removed in the same way. A large plant that is outgrowing its pot can be divided in spring. Roots and stems should be gently pulled into 2 sections, then repotted separately and kept at about 70°F (21°C), in shade, until they show signs of new growth. The Sail plant is a good plant to grow in hydroculture.

A healthy Sail plant has bright, glossy green leaves and, in summer, should show signs of new flowering stems among the leaves. Each flower lasts for 5 to 6 weeks, changing colour from white to green with age. As each one dies, it should be cut off at the base of its stem with sharp scissors. This encourages new flower stems to grow in its place.

Light: Semi-shade in summer, full light in winter. No direct summer sun.
Temperature: Winter minimum 55°F (13°C), though best at 60–65°F (16–18°C). Summer 65–70°F (18–21°C). If higher, humidity must also be high.
Water: 2–3 times a week in summer, once a week in winter, to keep moist at all times.
Humidity: Spray daily when temperature over 70°F (21°C); otherwise 3 times a week in summer, twice a week in winter. Stand pot on saucer of pebbles almost covered with water.
Feeding: Every 14 days in summer with liquid houseplant food diluted according to the maker's instructions.
Soil: 4 parts loam-based No. 3 and 1 part peat.
Repotting: Annually in spring as the plant starts into growth into next size 4 pot. Ensure good drainage in bottom of pot.
Cleaning: Wipe leaves with damp cloth. No leafshine.

Humidity
Sail plants need humidity all the year round. Spray daily if if over 70°F (21°C); if cooler, spray 3 times a week in summer, twice a week in winter. To provide permanent local humidity, stand pot on saucer of pebbles. Add water to saucer, almost covering pebbles but don't let base of pot touch water.

what goes wrong

Plant grows new leaves but produces no flowers. Either old, needs feeding or too dark. If 3–4 years old, divide plant. Needs full light in winter, semi-shade in summer. Feed every 14 days in summer.

Brown marks on flowers. Leafshine damage. Do not use.

Leaves and flowers droop and flop. Topsoil dry. Needs water. Water and spray more often to keep soil always moist in summer. If soil feels dry, plant too hot. Move to cooler place (under 70°F, 21°C if possible) and spray regularly.

Leaves yellow with webs underneath. Red spider mite. Spray every 14 days with diluted malathion or systemic insecticide until clear.

Leaves distorted and sticky with green insects. Greenfly. Spray with derris or pyrethrum every 14 days until clear.

Leaves go pale and slightly yellow. Too much direct summer sunlight. Move to shadier position.

Leaves dull, soft and rotten. Much too cold. Move to warmer place, 60–65°F (16–18°C) best in winter. Use tepid water for watering in winter and do not allow plant to dry out.

Leaves droop and flop. Top soil very wet with mould and rotting on surface. Much too wet, waterlogged. Check drainage hole in bottom of pot is clear. Allow plant to dry out completely before watering.

73

Stephanotis floribunda

Madagascar jasmine

Well-known for its waxy, bell-shaped scented white flowers, the essential constituent of most summer bridal bouquets, Madagascar jasmine is not an easy plant to grow in the home. It requires plenty of light and careful watering, especially in winter when too much can be fatal. It is best when allowed to climb up the walls of a greenhouse or conservatory where its clusters of blooms will hang down all summer. In the house, it can be trained up a cane or round a hoop and, in a good, light window, should grow successfully. In good conditions its shoots can grow 2ft (60cm) a year, eventually reaching 20ft or more (over 6m).

Madagascar jasmine has clusters of pretty white, waxy flowers among bright green leaves. When buying, look for a plant with healthy young buds, not those in full flower. In the home it needs a very good, light position out of direct midday sun and careful watering to keep it in good condition.

Light: Plenty. Place on sun-facing window-sill, shaded from mid-day sun in height of summer.
Temperature: Winter minimum 55°F (13°C); summer minimum 60°F (15°C), maximum 75°F (24°C).
Water: 2–3 times a week in summer, once a week in winter with tepid, soft water. Water less if temperature falls below minimum so that compost almost dries out.
Humidity: Spray daily in summer, once a week in winter with tepid soft water, avoiding clusters of flowers. Stand pot on saucer of pebbles almost covered with water. Do not allow base of pot to touch water.
Feeding: Every 14 days in spring and summer when growing and flowering with houseplant food diluted with water. Use half as much food as maker recommends.
Soil: Loam-based No. 1 compost.
Repotting: When young and very vigorous, repot twice a year in spring and summer. Annually in spring sufficient after 2 years.
Cleaning: Humidity spraying sufficient. If very dirty, wipe with damp cloth. No leafshine.

Brown spots on flowers. Leafshine damage. Do not use.

Brown scales on stems and under leaves. Scale insect. Paint with cotton wool dipped in methylated spirits or spray every 14 days with diluted malathion until clear.

74

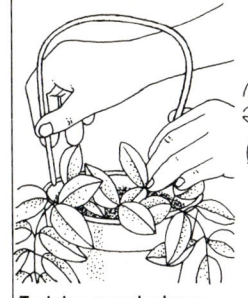

Training round a hoop
1. Push ends of wire hoop or thin cane so that they are ⅔ down pot on opposite sides. Bend plant stem to one side of hoop and gently twist around.

2. To secure plant to hoop, tie twine to one end of hoop and thread it along, looping it loosely around stem. Do not tie tight knots or stem may be damaged.

Leaves dull and limp, flowers dry up. Air too dry. Spray daily in summer, once a week in winter and stand pot on saucer of wet pebbles to provide extra humidity.

New leaves turn yellow. The effect of tap water. Water once with a weak solution of sequestered iron (use half the amount recommended on the bottle) then use only lime-free water.

Leaves turn yellow with webs underneath. Red spider mite. Spray every 14 days with diluted malathion until clear.

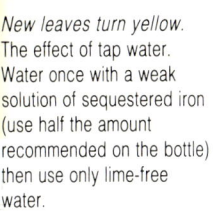

Flower buds shrivel. Too hot and dry. Move to cooler place (below 75°F, 24°C) if possible and water 2 to 3 times a week in summer to keep soil always moist.

Flower buds drop off without opening. Plant moved around too much or too cold. Keep in warmer place (60°F, 15°C at least in summer) and do not move plant around from place to place when it comes into flower.

what goes wrong

Leaves turn yellow and drop. Too dark or too wet, overwatered. Check conditions and move to lighter place. If compost very wet, allow to dry out before watering again.

White woolly patches on leaves and stems. Mealy bug. Remove with cotton wool dipped in methylated spirits or spray every 14 days with diluted malathion until clear.

75

Strelitzia reginae

Bird of Paradise flower

The exotic-looking Bird of Paradise flower is a slow grower and not difficult to keep going. Its grey-green leaves grow 18in (45cm) long and 5in (12cm) wide, on stems the same length. When about 4–5 years old, a long flower stem grows, ending in a flower pod which contains several orange and purple flowers. These come out one after the other during the summer. While not difficult to grow, it is very much a collector's plant and is not easy to obtain. Once in the home, however, it is a tough and long-lasting plant which deserves to be more widely grown. After many years, the plants form clumps which may be divided in spring. Each section should have at least 4 leaves and a good portion of root. The new plants should be kept in a warm place (70°F, 21°C) in good light (out of direct sun) and watered about once a week.

The Bird of Paradise flower's orange and purple blooms emerge one after the other from its beak-like flower pod. Its long leaves have a greyish, slightly matt finish which should not be removed with leafshine. Flower stems will not appear until the plant is 4–5 years old but will then come every year during the summer.

Light: Plenty, including full sunshine.
Temperature: Winter minimum 50°F (10°C), summer maximum 75°F (24°C).
Water: Up to 3 times a week in summer, once a week in winter, to keep soil moist but not waterlogged.
Humidity: Spray daily in summer, especially if near maximum temperature, avoiding drips of water on leaves. Spray weekly in winter.
Feeding: Every 10 days in summer with houseplant food diluted according to the maker's instructions.
Soil: Loam-based No. 3 compost.
Repotting: Annually in spring up to 4 years in next size pot. Then just change topsoil every year and feed.
Cleaning: Humidity spraying sufficient. If very dirty, wipe leaves with damp cloth. No leafshine.

Changing the topsoil
1. When plant is over 4 years old, keep in same pot but remove top inch (2½cm) soil in spring each year, taking care not to damage roots.

2. Replace with fresh compost and firm well around base of plant.

3. Water well and add dose of liquid houseplant food to give immediate nourishment.

76

what goes wrong

Leaves dry out. Too dry. Water up to 3 times a week in summer, once a week in winter, keeping soil moist.

Leaves blacken and curl. Too cold. Keep above 50°F (10°C) in winter. Do not allow leaves to touch glass in cold weather. Frost damage may be fatal but move to warmer place to see if plant recovers.

White woolly patches on leaves and stems. Mealy bug. Spray every 14 days with diluted malathion or wipe with cotton-wool dipped in methylated spirits.

Leaves shrivel and curl up. Too dark. Move to lighter place, including full sunshine.

Base of plant rots and blackens. Too wet. Check drainage in pot and allow soil to dry out before watering again. Water only about once a week in winter, allowing compost surface to dry out between waterings.

Brown scales under leaves and on stems. Scale insect. Spray every 14 days with malathion or remove with cotton-wool dipped in methylated spirits.

Vriesia splendens

Flaming sword

In the wild, this plant (a bromeliad) grows on the jungle trees of tropical South America. It is a striking plant, with a brilliant orange flower spike or spathe rising some 18in (45cm) out of the central rosette formed of horizontally striped dark brown and green leaves. The flower itself is small, yellow and looks rather like a lobster's claw coming out of the side of the spathe. One of the eaiest Bromeliads to grow, a Flaming sword plant provides a good contrast of shape and form in mixed plantings. Like other bromeliads, it dies down after flowering (2–2½ years) but produces new offsets at its base. When choosing a new plant, inspect its central well carefully. The spike should be just appearing, not fully grown with flowers, and certainly not already fading.

The Flaming sword produces its flower spike (below) when it is about 2 years old but even without a flower, is an attractive houseplant. Its striped green and brown leaves enclose a central well which must be kept full of clean, lime-free water.

Light: Good light position with some sunshine, though not full mid-day sun.
Temperature: Best to maintain constant 60°F (15°C). Winter minimum 55°F (13°C), summer maximum 70°F (21°C).
Water: Keep centre of rosette filled at all times, except when flower stem is appearing, changing water weekly. Water compost once a week in summer, keep drier in winter, watering every 10–14 days.
Humidity: Spray overhead weekly.
Feeding: Every 14 days in summer add liquid houseplant food to water for central well. Use half as much food as maker recommends.
Soil: Peat-based compost.
Repotting: Twice as plant grows to flowering size, i.e. at about 6-month intervals.
Cleaning: Wipe leaves with damp cloth. Do not use leafshine.

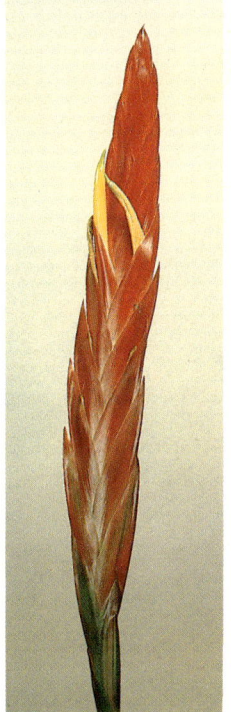

Brown scales under leaves. Scale insect. Remove with cotton-wool dipped in methylated spirits or spray every 14 days with systemic insecticide until clear.

what goes wrong

Leaves shrivel and tips turn brown. Too dry. Keep water in central rosette, changing every week. Water compost once a week in summer, once every 10 to 14 days in winter.

Removing the flower stem
When flower spike has died, cut its stem at base with secateurs.

Offsets
Offsets can be cut from the parent when they are about half the parent's size and have roots of their own. Separate with a sharp knife, making sure offset has its roots attached. Pot in new pot. Water and keep warm (75°F, 24°C).

Flower stem discoloured, flowers die as they come out. Leafshine damage. Do not use.

Leaves fade and become pale. Too dark. Move to position with good light. Will take some direct sun, though not hot mid-day sunlight.

Leaves shrivel up. Too hot. Keep under 70°F (21°C) in summer. Constant 60°F (15°C) ideal. If plant not moved to cooler place, may die.

Central rosette starts to die and young side shoots appear at base. This is natural after about 2 years. Do not remove young shoots until centre rosette of parent plant has died completely.

Leaves fade and have webs underneath. Red spider mite. Spray every 14 days with diluted malathion or derris.

Base of rosette rots. Too cold and too wet – usually fatal. Empty water from central well and allow soil to dry out. If it recovers and young side shoots appear, place in warmer position, 60°F (15°C).

Buying your houseplant

Florists, garden centres and specialist shops are best for unusual plants, large specimens and planted arrangements. Supermarkets, stores and service stations often offer excellent value in popular plants and rely on fast turnover to maintain quality. Market stalls may appear to offer good value but take care, especially in winter, when cold may affect the plants badly.

It is important before buying to consider where the plant is to go. Think about the room conditions, the light, heat or draughts that the plant may be subjected to. If you are a beginner choose a plant that is simple to grow. Don't be tempted to buy one that is exotic until you have had some experience.

Look carefully at the one you intend to buy. It should be firm in its pot, which should be clean. The compost on top should be fresh, not sprouting weeds or moss. None of the leaves should be marked, torn, yellow or faded. Beware of small plants in large pots; this probably means that they have just been repotted and the roots will not have grown properly into the fresh compost.

Always insist, particularly in winter, that the plant you buy is properly wrapped up, if necessary with a double layer of paper. Large plants often require support, with an extra cane to protect the growing tip. Take care not to knock it on the way home.

Lastly, make sure you know the plant's correct name so that you can look up its care instructions when you get home. Common names vary from place to place; the scientific name is the most reliable to use for identification.

Acknowledgements

Colour artwork by Stuart Lafford, Andrew Riley/The Garden Studio (pp. 24, 28, 44 and cover), John Wilkinson, (p. 67)

Line artwork by Patricia Newton (pp. 1–5), Andrew Robinson and Andrew MacDonald (pp. 6–78)

Photographs by David Cockroft

Plants by courtesy of Thomas Rochford & Son Ltd, Longmans Florists

Additional photographs supplied by the The Harry Smith Horticultural Photographic Collection and A-Z Botanical Photographic Collection

Designed by Marion Neville

Typeset by Faz Graphics